Literary Criticism in America

Literary Criticism in America

A Preliminary Survey

GEORGE E. DE MILLE

NEW YORK / RUSSELL & RUSSELL

FIRST PUBLISHED IN 1931
REISSUED, 1967, BY RUSSELL & RUSSELL
A DIVISION OF ATHENEUM HOUSE INC.
L. C. CATALOG CARD NO: 66–24685

MANUFACTURED IN THE UNITED STATES OF AMERICA

Finally it is a pleasant duty to record here my obligations to three scholars: William S. Knickerbocker, whose fertile suggestiveness first conceived the idea of this book; Jay Hubbell, whose sound judgment and thorough scholarship has so often kept me from wandering astray; and Matthew W. Rosa, whose constant friendship and encouragement has carried me through many a dark hour.

FOREWORD

"Why," some serious-minded person is sure to ask, "why bother to write a history of American literary criticism? Literature itself is life at second-hand; criticism is literature at second-hand; and criticism of criticism, therefore, is far removed indeed from anything vital or beautiful."

The readiest, and perhaps the most truthful answer would be, "Because it amused me to do so." But this, while certainly a sufficient justification for doing the job, is hardly a justification for thrusting it on a book-deluged public. I sincerely believe that there are good reasons for publishing such a book as this.

The relation between criticism and other forms of literature—for criticism, to be worth anything, must be in itself literature—is exceedingly intimate. As to the exact nature of that relation, many battles of words have been waged. There is the view of the minor poet, who, having been harshly treated by some critic of high standards and severe temper, cries out that criticism is the blight on creation, the enemy of all literary progress. This view is mere nonsense.

The second view is that the critic is a sort of literary schoolmaster, whose business it is to teach the writers how to write, and to rap them sharply over the knuckles when they fail to follow instructions. There is more of truth in this opinion. Boileau did apparently act as a sort of tutor to Racine. Dryden did, in his tragedies, attempt to follow religiously the rules of the Aristotelian critics of France and Italy. Whitman did respond, like an echo, to the prophetic call of Emerson. But it is instructive to note that during the Eighteenth Century, when this notion of criticism was everywhere prevalent, poetry and the drama, the two forms of literature with which criticism mainly concerned itself, steadily declined, while the essay and the novel, despised and neglected, grew apace. Clearly, then, this view does not contain the whole truth.

That there is, however, a relation, and that the relation is very close is, I think, amply proved by the fact that in every period of literary history of which we have anything like complete information, a time of great activity in the other kinds of creative writing has been also a time of great activity in criticism. Thus, the period of Shakespeare and Spenser and the whole company of Elizabethan poets and dramatists is also the period of Jonson and Sidney, of *Arts of Poesie* and *Defences of Rhyme* almost without number. The second flourishing of English drama in Restoration days is also the period of the magnificent critical work of Dryden. In the France of Louis XIV, the era of Corneille and Racine and Molière and La Fontaine was also the era of Boileau and Vaugelas and Fontenelle and Fénelon. The rise of Romantic poetry in England was paralleled by the rise of the Romantic criticism of Coleridge and Lamb and Hazlitt. The flowering of German literature in the days of Goethe and Schiller came in part as the result of a half-century of German critical activity, and coincided in time with the critical writing of the Schlegels. The age of Hugo in France was also the age of Sainte-Beuve. And to come to American literature, the decade which saw the beginnings of the New England school of writers also ushered in the critical work of Lowell and Poe. We might almost generalize, and state that every important school of creative writers has had its critical spokesman.

But the critic is in the main neither policeman nor pedagogue, though he may at times assume the functions of these civic worthies. His relation to the creator is something more subtle than that. To attempt a definition of that relation, one must leave the solid ground of historical fact, and venture forth on the quicksands of conjecture. I offer the following view for what it is worth. The man who sits down to write a book has, I believe, always a public in mind—not that vague entity, the general public, but a public of a very specific and limited sort. He writes to secure the approval of a class, a group, or even a single man. Shakespeare is generally conceived to have been as indifferent to critical opinion, to rules and theories of literature, as any writer who ever lived. And yet, as Brander Matthews has pointed out, *The Tempest* complies, with an exactness that can be the result of no mere accident, with the so-called Aristotelian unities as formulated by Shakespeare's friend, Ben Jonson.

Now the excellence of a writer will in part, perhaps a very great part, be determined by the kind of public he has in mind while writing. If he writes for typists and clerks in gents' furnishing stores, the result will be something like *When a Man's a Man,* or the poems of Edgar Guest. When he writes for a more intellectual public, he may, if the gods favor him, produce *North of Boston,* or *The Song of the Lark.* And it is the special function of the critic to speak for the civilized minority, for that restricted public which is interested in literature as an art, which has intelligent opinions about books and a discriminating taste. It is his business to make the writer sensible of the pressure of a civilized body of opinion, and to make him write, therefore, more carefully, more artfully, more beautifully. The critic may accomplish this by the method of castigation; he will probably accomplish it more effectively by expressing an intelligent appreciation, by setting up instructive comparisons, by all the apparatus at the command of the sympathetic and discriminating critic.

If all this is true, and I firmly believe it is, it follows therefore that we cannot fully understand a writer unless we are aware of the critical currents which flowed about him, changing and shaping his work. No one, I venture to say, can begin to comprehend the changes that have taken place, in our own time, in such writers as Booth Tarkington and Sinclair Lewis—I use as illustrations writers as far apart as possible—unless he knows something of the critical opinion which brought about that change.

Within the last two decades, one of the main activities of the American mind has been the study of its own past. The main effort of American scholars has been directed toward the breaking down of erroneous and traditional estimates in all the fields of American history—political, social, economic, literary. This has involved a corresponding process of rediscovery and revaluation. The total result is that practically every American history written prior to 1915 is of value today only as a mine of facts. This is particularly true of the histories of American literature. One of our chief intellectual needs at the present time is a new history of American literature incorporating the results of the very considerable labors of scholars in that field in the past few years. But if my view of literary criticism and its relations to other branches of literary endeavor has anything of truth in it, such a history cannot be written until a thorough study has been made of the history of literary criticism in America. Up to the present time, no such study has been made.[1] In the hope, then, that this first, and therefore of necessity imperfect survey may be of some use to future students in this field, I humbly submit it.

[1] I shall have frequent occasion to refer to Norman Foerster's *American Criticism* (1928), a book with which I often disagree in detail, but which is the best connected study of American literary criticism that has yet been made. It is not a history, but a detailed examination of four great critics, Lowell, Poe, Emerson, and Whitman.

CONTENTS

CHAPTER PAGE

I THE NORTH AMERICAN REVIEW 17

II LOWELL 49

III POE 86

IV EMERSON AND MARGARET FULLER 118

V STEDMAN 133

VI HENRY JAMES 158

VII HOWELLS 182

VIII HUNEKER 206

IX SHERMAN 245

X EPILOGUE 277

Literary Criticism in America

CHAPTER I

The North American Review

I

Unlike all respectable, normally constituted literatures, American literature grew up backwards. In most other countries, there is a fairly regular temporal sucession of literary forms; epic gives way to lyric, drama follows, prose history is born, and finally the essay and the novel appear. But in American literature, our two earliest literary men of any permanent value are Cooper the novelist and Irving the essayist. American drama begins in the very late Nineteenth Century, and the American epic is still in the womb of time. And it is almost the truth that we have an American literary criticism before we have an American literature to criticize.

To all intents and purposes, literary criticism in America begins in the year 1815.[1] It began in Bos-

[1] Before that time, Brockden Brown and Joseph Dennie did some slight work in the critical field, but their work was neither important nor influential.

ton, of course. In the winter of 1814, there was in that city an organization known as the Anthology Club, composed mainly of clergymen and lawyers, graduates of Harvard College, interested in literature, and highly patriotic. It galled their souls, naturally enough, to be compelled to turn for news of what was going on in the literary world to that organ of British arrogance, the *Edinburgh Review*. The fathers of these men had fought at Concord and Bunker Hill for the political independence of the United States. It was obviously the duty of their valiant sons to establish a like independence in the world of literature. And the first step toward that desired, but possibly not even yet attained end, was the foundation of an American review.

Willard Phillips, A. H. Everett, R. H. Dana, Walter Channing, John Gorham Palfrey—names aromatic of Boston, old Harvard College, and a sound classical culture—were the leaders in the project. To them came William Tudor, a gentleman of commercial interests, fresh from Europe, filled with plans of his own for an American rival of the *Edinburgh*. In May, 1815, under the editorship of Mr. Tudor, the first number of the *North American Review* was issued.

It was an interesting production, this grandfather

of American magazines.[2] A glance through its time-yellowed pages carries us back a hundred years, straight into the heart of a past—not that past as exhumed in a mummified condition by the researches of historians, but the past alive, explaining itself in its own living voice.

The magazine opens with an article, the first of a long series, on "Books Relating to North America"—the patriotic motive at work. This is followed by letters to the editor, dealing with such burning topics as "The Hours of Public Worship," "The Improvement of Mail Coaches," and "The Modern Love of Scandal." There is a violent attack on the *Edinburgh* for its violent attacks on America. There is a review of *Moral Pieces in Prose and Verse*, by Miss Lydia Huntly. There is an extended notice of the endowment of a Professorship of Greek in Harvard College. Finally, there is a list of books newly published in America—mainly controversial theology and piratings from England. In succeeding issues, there are accounts of the proceedings of the American Academy of Arts and Sciences; there are addresses delivered before the Phi Beta Kappa Society; there are occasional sermons. Harvard and its

[2] A grandfather who survived many of his grandchildren. The *North American* is still in existence.

news, indeed, supply a good part of the material in these early volumes—volumes over which one can see solemn, white-haired old gentlemen, graduates of the college, pillars of the Old South Church, seated in quiet studies on Beacon Street, nodding their heads in grave approval.

Like most editors who cannot pay for contributions, Mr. Tudor very nearly had to write his own magazine. About three-fourths of the first volume flowed from his prolific pen. In his first critical article, the review of Miss Huntly's *Moral Pieces* noted above, there is one sentence that deserves quotation.

> The whole of the passage ending with the lines,
> 'No slightest breath her bosom cheered,
> Her own soft wings alone she heard.'
> If not sublime, which we think it to be, will at least be allowed by all to be exquisitely beautiful and pathetic.

Three more reviews, dealing with Scott and Leigh Hunt, are from Mr. Tudor's pen. They lack the note of distinction that characterizes the first; they are merely dull. But Tudor's longest and most ambitious article, "On Models in Literature" is in the main a plea, both sensible and patriotic, for a native American literature, truly native, not borrowed. In the service of originality, it deals hard blows at the prevailing Latinolatry, and its remarks on the advisability of discarding models and returning to nature, while conventional enough, were sorely needed reminders. But Mr. Tudor's talents were rather commercial than critical, and in 1816 he left the *Review* to finish his days in the consular service.

For the next fifteen years, the *Review* remained in the hands of its founders. They formed a close corporation, and though the editorial title was passed from hand to hand, the *Review* throughout this period is the work of the group as a whole. Only one of the circle, R. H. Dana, Senior, was a professional man of letters, and in many respects he stands apart from his fellows. The true representatives were Jared Sparks, clergyman and biographer; E. T. Channing, lawyer and professor; Willard Phillips, lawyer; A. H. Everett, clergyman; J. G. Palfrey, clergyman and historian; and Edward Everett, clergyman, professor, orator, and statesman. The work of these men is so homogeneous that one can almost treat them as a sort of composite critic. Alike in antecedents, in training, in social background, in theological opinions, they are singularly alike in literary creed. Furthermore, they were writing for a small and homogeneous public. Their work is marked throughout by one set of attitudes, opinions, prejudices, judgments. Never were critics more certain of themselves. They knew who counted among contemporary writers. There were exactly four great living English poets—Byron, Campbell, Wordsworth, Scott. As to the precise ranking of these poets, there is some doubt. Byron is generally the favorite for first place, in spite of his personal profligacy and literary licentiousness. Moore, whom one must consider, since he is so astoundingly popular, is thoroughly bad, both as a man and as a poet. That there were other Englishmen writing passable poetry at this time, our reviewers never realized. It is not until 1829 that the names of Coleridge, Keats, and Shelley appear in the pages of the *Review,* and then they are merely mentioned as gentlemen who have written some verse.

In the novel, the field of serious critical consideration was even more limited. While one was compelled at times to review the ephemeral—*Demetrius, Anastasius, Yamoyden, a Tale,* are among the titles—one's serious admiration is reserved for two and only two novelists—Scott and Edgeworth. Particularly is this noticeable in the critical writings of A. H. Everett. To him, Scott is a veritable King

Charles's head. Whether he discusses Voltaire or Byron, the tales of St. Pierre or the literary tendencies of the Eighteenth Century, he always drags in Scott.

In spite, however, of their admiration for Byron, Scott, and Wordsworth, the fathers of the review were by no means Romantic in their literary doctrines. They are indeed a clear illustration of the late survival of the Eighteenth Century in America. In 1817, a year before the appearance of *Endymion,* Willard Phillips could still assert, with a dogmatic certainty worthy of Bysshe, that the heroic couplet is the greatest of all English meters. Typical of the minor critics of the Eighteenth Century is the following group of assertions.

In addition to that strong sense of natural beauty, without which no man can be a poet, he has shown throughout a vein of true pathos, without which the most splendid poetry soon grows tiresome. The sentiments are often fine and striking, always just, noble, and generous.

And as late as 1830, I find one critic declaring, with the air of one who states a commonplace,

Pope carried the sustained harmony and sweetness of English versification to a degree unexcelled before. It is difficult to detect much that is delicate and harmonious in the earlier English poets. The rhymes of Chaucer form no exception to this remark.

Writing for a New England public, with over half of their number clerics, the reviewers were naturally somewhat inclined to take a moral view of literature. Even Mr. Tudor, the commercial critic, declaims in an aside against "the wild licentiousness of our times." And he is a liberal. Of his six sucessors, three were clergymen. They congratulate themselves, therefore, that "the theory which treats of beauty, as of something independent of moral effect is still without advocates among us." They regret that "the moral effect of the drama has not in general been of the most exalted kind." They are glad to find a novel "replete with profound practical wisdom, conveyed in a vigorous and massy style." Dogmatically they pronounce that "there can be no more hideous fault in a literary work than profligacy. Levity is next in order." They wish that Shakespeare might have followed Spenser's excellent example, and furthered virtue by poetry, instead of wasting his time depicting "the essentially coarse and vulgar mind of Falstaff."

As I have pointed out, the patriotic motive was one of the chief reasons for founding the *Review*.

The magazine naturally became, then, the first literary advocate of hundred-per-cent Americanism. Our critics, anticipating Emerson and Whitman, are continually calling for an American literature to appear—a really American literature, smacking of the soil, purged of old-world influences. With a curious national inferiority complex, they are continually resenting the slights of the *Edinburgh,* and at the same time aping that publication most sedulously. They attempt the same magisterial air; they have the same trick of making a book review the text for a sermon on things in general. And they are continually pointing out, to that same contemptuous magazine, that there *is* an American literature, numbering among its classics Thomas Jefferson, Fisher Ames, and the Rev. Dr. Buckminster.

But although temptingly easy, it is hardly fair to poke fun at the strenuous strivings of these estimable gentlemen. They had a difficult work to do, a work that needed doing, and in their peculiar way they accomplished a great deal. They felt themselves to be—and they were—the schoolmasters of a new literature. Everett's numerous articles on French literature, Prescott's Italian discoveries, all helped to introduce these literatures to a raw American public. They were often wrong, and sometimes positively silly, in their particular literary opinions. But in that day, to take literature seriously enough to write about it, even though one wrote foolishly; to make a money-grubbing Yankee public aware that Wordsworth and Scott were writing abroad, and that Irving and Cooper and Bryant were beginning to produce literature here in America; to provide a forum for the expression of literary opinion; to form and train that most necessary of things for the production of literature, a reading public—this was to have done something worthy of a monument. Willard Phillips's heroic couplet heresy is more than atoned for by his publication of *Thanatopsis*.

In its earliest days, the tendency of the *Review* was to err on the side of leniency toward American books. This was natural, and hardly blameable. The magazine was an experiment, its very life a fragile and delicate thing. It could not afford to make enemies within its own public. And so, for two or three years, it hailed with joy every American book that appeared. Bryant's review of the history of American poetry, published in 1818, marks the beginning of a more discriminating criticism. Bryant knew good poetry from bad; he had even as a young man a certain severity of temper; and he did not hesitate to call a poem worthless. And indeed, most of the material with which he had to deal was worthless.

In 1822 *The Spy* appeared, and was reviewed early in the next year. This review, by an author outside the original *North American* group, I find superior in its judgment of Cooper to many criticisms written much later and by critics of far greater fame. The author, whom I take to have been the John Sylvester Gardiner, who was rector of Trinity, Boston, from 1805 to 1830, was, of all the contributors to the *Review* during the first decade of its existence, by far the best critic. The mere fact that, in that day, he dared to specialize in the novel shows something of his quality. His views on Cooper were sound, a judicious mixture of praise and blame. His attacks on the bad novels of the period are both vigorous and lively. His long essay on *Novel Writing* shows surprising divergences from the orthodox Scott-Edgeworth cult. He actually praises realism. And he ventures to say, in the face of the persisting neo-classic dogma of the hierarchy of literary forms, that the novel is superior to the epic, since it is more real. He is even weak on the moral side; he approves of Shakespeare's lack of moral teaching.

There is one other man who stands apart from the group with which he was associated—R. H. Dana, Senior. Dana is the only man of these early days of the *Review* whose name is still remembered. Unlike his associates—clergymen, lawyers, teachers, to whom literature was little more than an elegant relaxation—Dana was something like a professional man of letters. And he struck a note of his own. While his friends were still writing and thinking in the Eighteenth Century, while Pope and the heroic couplet still reigned in literary Boston, Dana was preaching high Romanticism. As early as 1819 he dared to assert—and it was an assertion that must have taken courage,—that Pope, the monarch of English poetry, was not a poet at all. The origin of that faith is evident. Dana's critical ancestry is further shown by his inflated Shelley-and-water disquisitions on the high spiritual virtues of poetry. He is a thorough Wordsworthian in his praise of nature and the simple life; he even borrows Wordsworth's dislike of Thomson, convicted of the crime of using poetic diction. He speaks highly of the criticism of Coleridge, though he gives no indication of following that great critical leader. In spite of these romantic elements, however, he still believes in "The Rules," and we find him attacking Hazlitt because that unsystematic person will make a new definition of poetry to fit every new poet he reads. But his greatest errors arise when he comes to discuss prose style. The two authors whom he particularly attacks on grounds of style are Hazlitt and Irving. Some of the attributes of a critic Dana had—genuine love for literature, independence of judgment, a fresh view-point, at least for his time and country. But like nearly all the American critics of his age, he was more interested in many other things than in literature. After 1820, he plunged into the Unitarian controversy, and was lost to criticism.

About 1824, three younger writers began to make themselves heard in the columns of the *Review*. F. W. P. Greenwood, Harvard graduate and Unitarian clergyman, was separated from the older group by differences in age and in critical viewpoint. He first appears in the *Review* as the author of an article on Wordsworth. Defective, old-fashioned, this article is nevertheless noteworthy for two things. Greenwood points out, clearly and sharply, that Wordsworth's unpopularity was largely due to his logical carrying-out of his peculiar theory of poetry. And to account for his other shortcomings, Greenwood merely remarks, with a sensible brevity that is refreshing after the wordy labyrinths of Dana, "He talks too much." Plain speaking like that was rare in those days of critical dignity and critical dullness. There was a promise in Greenwood, but again it was a promise unfulfilled. The moral complex was too strong for him, and he joined the anti-Byronists—Everett, Andrews Norton, Phillips—whose constant attacks on Byron formed one of the few exciting features of the *Review*. Thus, Greenwood denounced Pinkney, not because Pinkney was a second-hand poet, not because he imitated, but because he imitated Byron, rather than worthier and more upright models. In like fashion, Greenwood approved highly of Hillhouse's *Hadad,* that "ornament and bright addition to the literature of our country," mainly because the scene of the poem is laid in Palestine, and its characters bear resounding biblical names.

About the same time began the long connection with the *Review* of the Peabody brothers—Oliver William Bourn and William Bourn Oliver. Prolific and long-lived, they carried on the traditions of the earliest *North American* group twenty years after the last member of the original Anthology Club had ceased to write.

II

In 1831, A. H. Everett became editor of the *Review,* and with his assumption of office came a new phase in the magazine's existence. The original group, the founders, was dying out. By 1830 Dana, Phillips, Sparks, and Channing had ceased writing, and Everett did little criticism during his editorship. Times were changing, and the *Review* was changing with them.

The decade was a period of awakening in American literature. A mere inspection of the titles of the books reviewed during these years is a lesson in literary history. One feels the strivings and stirrings of a literature becoming adolescent. There had been American authors before. But except for Cooper and Irving, every American writer whose books had come before the critics for review during the first fifteen years of the magazine's existence is today either completely buried and forgotten, or preserved only in the alcohol of historical research. The great American novelist prior to 1830, if greatness is measured by space in the reviews, was Catherine Sedgewick. Has anyone alive read *Hope Leslie,* or *The Linwoods?* She still wrote in the thirties, but she had rivals—Nathaniel Hawthorne, for one, whose *Twice Told Tales* made a very slight stir in 1837. Dana was superseded as poet laureate by Longfellow, the particular favorite of the *Review*, Whittier and Holmes and Lowell were making themselves felt. Emerson had begun his assault on Puritan orthodoxy. American literature was awake.

With 1830, it becomes more difficult to make sweeping generalizations concerning the *Review*. The critics of the earlier time can be treated together because of their remarkable unanimity of opinion. But through the thirties there were neither sharply defined groups nor dominating figures. However, certain tendencies can be made out.

The Eighteenth Century was slowly passing away. The Peabodies continued to uphold the good old traditions. It was Oliver who was still saying in 1830 that English poetry began with Pope. In 1832 Prescott, writing a comprehensive survey of English literature since 1800, did not feel impelled to mention the names of Keats, Coleridge, or Shelley. But these are survivals. The prevailing trend of the times is better represented by an article, published in 1834, in which Coleridge is hailed as the greatest music-maker in English verse since the Elizabethans. This article, the sole contribution of R. C.

Waterston—who he was I have been unable to discover—is the finest bit of poetical criticism in the *Review* up to its date. In the same year Oliver Peabody wrote on Crabbe in a manner to atone for some of his many critical sins. In 1835, Everett introduced the American public to Carlyle, who was still a joke to many British critics. And C. C. Felton, Professor of Greek at Harvard and friend of Longfellow, discarding the Eighteenth Century canons of criticism, ventured to make use of Coleridge's three critical questions.

Emerson's *Milton,* which appeared in 1838, is the first bit of prose in the *Review* which is itself literature; but it is an isolated phenomenon. Of the critics of this decade, one only deserves treatment individually—Henry Wadsworth Longfellow. Of Longfellow as a critic, pure and simple, one cannot think very highly. He has left us one article only on contemporary literature—a review of *Twice Told Tales.* In eight pages, Longfellow manages to convey just three ideas regarding the tales; they are poetic, national in subject, and written in a beautiful style.[3] Much more useful is the article on Sidney's *Defence of Poesie.* The article really consti-

[3] By removing from this eight page article just forty-eight words, one can make it impossible for a reader to tell either the author or the book under consideration.

tutes Longfellow's own apology for poetry. I know of nothing which impresses one more fully with the anti-literary character of the American public in the early Nineteenth Century than the fact that nearly every critic of poetry, and nearly every writer of poetry during the period, found it necessary to apologize for poetry, to plead for it on moral and utilitarian grounds. They sound obvious, almost silly, these poetic defences of Lowell and Dana and Longfellow; but they are evidently written to meet a very definite need. It is interesting to note Longfellow's case for the defence.

> Poetry neither enervates the mind nor unfits it for the practical duties of life.
>
> Nor is it less true, that the legitimate tendency of poetry is to exalt, rather than to debase—to purify, rather than to corrupt.

This article is the prelude to a series of five, the mere titles of which are significant.

The Origin and Progress of the French Language
History of the Italian Language and Dialects
Spanish Moral and Devotional Poetry
Spanish Language and Literature
Tegner's Frithiof's Saga

These are not so much criticism as education and propaganda. The first of the series is practically an introduction to mediæval French Literature in a simplified form. Like an elementary text, it begins with the Strasburg Oaths; it is filled with quotations and examples, noteworthy among them Longfellow's own renderings from the Troubadours. Similar in nature and in aim are the other articles of the series; all of them important as beginnings of that cult of mediæval literature which has produced some of our finest American literary scholarship. For this work of introducing mediæval literature to the American public Longfellow was excellently qualified. He was not too good a scholar; he never became enough of a mediævalist to turn mystic or Catholic, and so frighten his public away. His intellectual nearness in so many respects to his public is an excellent second to the enthusiasm which is his most valuable critical quality. He often falls into pitfalls [4] but he is alive. His work stands out from the solemn, dreary pages of Felton and Henry Ware, illuminated by the light of his zeal.

III

The third period in the early history of the *North American Review* began in 1843, when Francis

[4] "Rabelais soon fatigues even the most quaint and curious."

Bowen became editor. Bowen had traveled abroad, and had managed to acquire on foreign soils a somewhat more liberal and literary spirit than had actuated his predecessors. He had himself many of the qualities of the literary critic. He loved a row, and in his consulship the *Review,* which under Everett had grown duller and duller year by year, took on a livelier tone. It was under Bowen that Poe and Felton fell to blows; Felton, who earned immortality by applying to Poe the epithet "forcible-feeble." Bowen was moreover a militant patriot. Significantly, his second critical article was a review—unfavorable—of Cooper's *Homeward Bound*. This was followed by a rousing, swashbuckling reply, in "The Morals, Manners, and Poetry of England," to British criticism of America. But Bowen was not content to fight foreign foes only. He even ventured to turn his critical guns on natives of sacred Boston. He vigorously attacked Channing and Emerson; he rapped Lowell over the knuckles when Lowell was one of the *Review's* most promising young contributors. "We are forgetting the object of our sermon—which is to teach poets to mind their own concerns, and not to quarrel with the world or the critics." All that because Lowell had ventured, in a review of Browning, to protest against the current methods of criticizing poetry.

Bowen's critical writings were mostly concerned with the novel. In his travels abroad, he had acquired a taste for French fiction—a taste that worked havoc with the moral tone of his criticism. Writing of the novels of Paul de Kock, he did feel it necessary to deprecate the Frenchman's morality, but that stands little in the way of his real enjoyment of the novels. Of Dumas he held the opinion, which has passed into orthodox teaching, that Dumas is greater as dramatist than as novelist. Dickens he early acclaimed, though disagreeing sharply with the *American Notes*. Fair critic, better editor, Bowen fathered a group of young men, the literary radicals of their day. With their help he filled the arteries of the *Review*, which during the thirties had begun to assume a corpse-like aspect, with fresh and coursing blood.[5]

To this group of literary radicals John Lothrop Motley belongs, by virtue of one article. But that article, a study of Balzac, was as radical a document in its way as the Preface to the *Lyrical Ballads*, and a direct counterblast to nine-tenths of the criticism of the novel written in America up to that time.

[5] Bowen was in the main a clever and intelligent reactionary, with certain strains of radicalism running through his mind.

Declaring roundly that he envied the French their freedom of speech in literature, Motley dared to commend Balzac for being a novelist who strove to be neither moral nor nasty, but who wrote from a detached and profound observation of the human spectacle. "Certainly the world should be reformed," Motley exclaimed, "but not by novel writers." The fathers of the *Review* must have turned in their graves.

Under Bowen, Lowell first joined the forces of the *Review,* as a rather fresh and flippant young poet-reformer. Of him we shall have much more to say later.

But the man who more than any other gave the critical pitch of the *Review* during the forties was Edwin Percy Whipple. Whipple has been almost forgotten, yet he is of great historical importance, since with him and with his part contemporary, Poe, criticism in America first became self-conscious. Before this time, it had been merely incidental and accidental, the leisure occupation of cultured gentlemen. But with Poe and Whipple, criticism was both a business and an art. They knew what they were doing.

Whipple was, I think, the first instance of the

self-educated man in American letters. Early left an orphan, he had no college training; began, unpromisingly enough, as a bank clerk; and developed into a lecturer and a librarian. The impress of this career is visible in his writing. His essay on Macaulay reveals clearly enough his critical master, standing out as it does from the prevailing stodginess of clerical and professorial critics by its directness and vigor. He writes of Macaulay in the Macaulayan manner. In this essay we find a foreshadowing of all the virtues and defects Whipple was to manifest as a critic. It is sharply written, keen in characterization, filled with enthusiasm for its subject. But it is occupied wholly with Macaulay the stylist and historian. It shows no understanding of Macaulay's almost complete failure to write understandingly of pure literature.

Whipple early acquired Macaulay's trick of making the ostensible subject of his reviews a mere point of departure for lengthy disquisitions on any topic, related or unrelated, on which it pleased him to speak. Thus his first article, which pretends to be a review of the critical work of Thomas Talfourd, is really an outline of British periodical criticism in the first quarter of the Nineteenth Century. It reveals two important things—Whipple's interest in criticism for its own sake, and his journalistic tendency.

His next attempt, a review of Griswold's *Poets and Poetry of America,* was less fortunate in its subject matter. It contains some extraordinary dicta. Mr. Dana is our most original poet. Pinkney is as good a lyrist as any of the Cavalier school.[6] "The Psalm of Life" is heroic, and with Longfellow in general, "the thought is more important than the manner of saying it." It is quite possible here, however, that Whipple has hit upon the truth, and that the conventional opinion that Longfellow was an excellent technician with no depth of thought, is wrong. But these remarkable statements are partly balanced by Whipple's recognition of the fact that *The Spanish Student* is a poem, not a play, and by Whipple's apt characterization of the early Whittier as too hot and over-fluent.

A series of minor articles followed, culminating in a long discussion of the British critics of the early Romantic period. This article, which appeared in 1845, is in many respects Whipple's critical masterpiece. Whipple had himself the judicial ideal of criticism. He had the hardness of head which is a prime

[6] George Saintsbury has commented on this strange saying.

requisite of a critic of criticism. He had an ear for prose, and he had himself a style in which to express his ideas—Macaulayan, keen-edged, always thoroughly alive. He was close enough to the Edinburgh Reviewers to understand their point of view, enough like them in temperament to write of them with appreciation, yet far enough removed to see clearly their curious errors of judgment. The essay is the work of a man who recognized criticism as a separate branch of literature, who had a definite notion of what criticism ought to be, and a keen mind to apply this ideal to the criticism he read. But perhaps Whipple's most pleasant quality was his evident appreciation of all writers, greater and lesser, from Byron to Sydney Smith, who were mentally alive and who wrote in a living style.

After this article came a group dealing with the great poets of the age just passing—Wordsworth, Byron, Shelley—and constituting a survey of English poetry in the early Nineteenth Century. They are strongly differentiated from the work of the whole line of American critics who had earlier dealt with these same men. Whipple was the earliest critic in American literature, as far as I know, to give any evidence of possessing the historical sense in literature, the first to look at movements, periods, not merely to inspect individuals. He was therefore the first to recognize—he may have learned something of this from Macaulay—the real significance of the Romantic movement. He did not commit the crime of talking about Wordsworth, Coleridge, and Campbell. He noted that principle of literary history, the alternation of periods. He attempted to trace—faintly foreshadowing Taine—the effect of the French Revolution on the Romantic Movement. He saw his writers against a background. Now, all this sounds commonplace enough; it was no commonplace, but startling originality, in the America of 1845.

In fact, Whipple was a radical. Of course, a radical in 1845 and a radical in 1929 are two different things. Whipple would not be ranked highly dangerous by existing standards. He was a New Englander, provided with the usual baggage of moral ideas that the New Englander of 1845 carried about with him. But to find a critic of that day, when the world bloomed with Unitarian hopefulness, objecting to "rose-colored moral sentiments" in an author is surprising. Still more surprising is Whipple's evident sympathy with such iconoclasts as Shelley and Byron. The earlier critics were unanimous about it; Byron was a great poet and a bad man. But it was

Byron the revolutionary to whom Whipple's heart went out. In fact, throughout these essays, the emphasis is laid on the personality of the poet, not on the quality of the poetry. And that brings us to Whipple's greatest critical defect. When he came to talk about men like Keats and Coleridge and Spenser—men who are merely poets and who write poetry that is merely poetry—Whipple had nothing to say. He cared, I suspect, very little about mere poetry, mere literature. He was rather lacking on the aesthetic side, though thoroughly alive on the intellectual.

He was, then, a lesser Macaulay. He had Macaulay's gift for skinning bad authors. He was always vigorous, original, alive. He could deal competently with a novelist, or a personality, or a period. And for all his weakness on the side of the purely beautiful, he was by all odds the greatest critic writing in the *North American* during our period, the only critic of the period who still retains any value.

By 1850, the *Review* had grown up. It is difficult to over-estimate the work it had done through these thirty-five years in fostering a genuine literary criticism in America. It had established a forum for the expression of critical opinion. It had pointed the way for other literary magazines—the *Southern*

Literary Messenger, *Graham's Magazine*, the *New York Mirror*. It had welcomed American authors and I think made a real contribution to their achievement by setting before them a body of critical opinion. It had seen the prevailing ideas in criticism change from those of the Eighteenth Century to the newer doctrines of the Romantic movement, and had itself helped in that change. It had given an opportunity to the best critical minds in the America of its day, and had set on their road at least two critics of value, Whipple and Lowell. It had made literary criticism in America an established fact.

REPRESENTATIVE CRITICAL ARTICLES APPEARING IN THE NORTH AMERICAN REVIEW, 1815–1850

Miss Huntley's *Poems*	William Tudor	May, 1815
The Lord of the Isles	William Tudor	July, 1815
On Models in Literature	William Tudor	March, 1816
Moore's *Lalla Rookh*	Walter Channing	November, 1817
Rob Roy	E. T. Channing	January, 1818
Brown's *Essay on American Poetry*	W. C. Bryant	July, 1818
Hazlitt's English Poets	R. H. Dana, Sr.	March, 1819
The Sketch Book	R. H. Dana, Sr.	September, 1819
Geoffroy on Dramatic Literature	A. H. Everett	April, 1820
Yamoyden	J. G. Palfrey	April, 1921
Bryant's Poems	Willard Phillips	October, 1821
Byron's Letter on Pope	W. H. Prescott	October, 1821
Percival's Poems	Edward Everett	January, 1822

The Spy	W. H. Gardiner[1]	July, 1822
French and English Tragedy	W. H. Prescott	January, 1823
Wordsworth's Poems	F. W. P. Greenwood	April, 1824
The Wilderness	W. H. Gardiner	July, 1824
Italian Narrative Poetry	W. H. Prescott	October, 1824
Lord Byron	A. H. Everett	January, 1825
Redwood, a Tale	W. C. Bryant	April, 1825
Recent American Novels	Jared Sparks	July, 1825
Lord Byron's Character and Writings	Andrews Norton	October, 1825
Hillhouse's *Hadad*	F. W. P. Greenwood	January, 1826
Cooper's Novels	W. H. Gardiner	July, 1826
Novel Writing	W. H. Gardiner	July, 1827
The Decline of Poetry	W. B. O. Peabody	January, 1829
Pelham	Willard Phillips	April, 1829
Moore's *Life of Byron*	W. B. O. Peabody	July, 1830
Studies in Poetry	O. W. B. Peabody	October, 1830
Origin and Progress of the French Language	H. W. Longfellow	April, 1831
Anglo-Saxon Language and Literature	H. W. Longfellow	October, 1831
Defence of Poetry	H. W. Longfellow	January, 1832
English Literature of the Nineteenth Century	W. H. Prescott	July, 1832
Early Literature of France	A. H. Everett	April, 1834
Life and Writings of Crabbe	O. W. B. Peabody	July, 1834
Coleridge's Poems	R. C. Waterston	October, 1834
Petrarch	G. W. Greene	January, 1835

[1] These initials, given in Poole, are certainly wrong. I allow them to stand, with the conjecture that they conceal J. S. Gardiner.

Willis's Writings	C. C. Felton	October, 1836
Hawthorne's *Twice Told Tales*	H. W. Longfellow	July, 1837
Cooper's Novels and Travels	Francis Bowen	January, 1838
Periodical Essays of the Age of Anne	W. E. Channing	April, 1838
Milton	R. W. Emerson	July, 1838
Hyperion	C. C. Felton	January, 1840
English Poetry in the Nineteenth Century	O. W. B. Peabody	April, 1840
Works of George Sand	Francis Bowen	July, 1841
Longfellow's Poems	C. C. Felton	July, 1842
Paul De Kock's Novels	Francis Bowen	April, 1843
Talfourd's Miscellaneous Writings	E. P. Whipple	October, 1843
Griswold's *Poets and Poetry of America*	E. P. Whipple	January, 1844
James's Novels	E. P. Whipple	April, 1844
New Translations of the Writings of Miss Bremer	J. R. Lowell	April, 1844
The Morals, Manners, and Poetry of England	Francis Bowen	July, 1844
Characteristics of Lord Byron	E. P. Whipple	January, 1845
The British Critics	E. P. Whipple	October, 1845
Nine New Poets	Francis Bowen	April, 1847
The New Timon	J. R. Lowell	April, 1847
Novels of Balzac	J. L. Motley	July, 1847
The *Knickerbocker* on Felton's *Agammemnon*	F. Bowen	July, 1847
Longfellow's *Evangeline*	C. C. Felton	January, 1848

THE NORTH AMERICAN REVIEW

Lowell's Poems	F. Bowen	April, 1848
Novels of the Season	E. P. Whipple	October, 1848
Charles Dickens	E. P. Whipple	October, 1849

NOTE ON WHIPPLE'S LATER WORKS

Whipple is one of those men who are not important enough to deserve a chapter, but too important to be left with mere passing mention. In 1848 he collected in two volumes his essays from the *North American.* These are the best volumes of criticism published in book form in America at that date. His next work, *Lectures on the Age of Elizabeth,* published in 1859, shows a great falling off. It is interesting as showing the response of a critic who was not a professional scholar to the movement for the study of older English literature. It is not a bad piece of work; it shows a surprisingly thorough reading in its period; it gives rather interesting sketches of the personalities of the Elizabethan writers. But the vigor of the earlier volume had pretty much died out; the faint pink radicalism had faded; the originality was all gone. Like nine-tenths of the books on the Elizabethan age written during the last century, it is only Charles Lamb over again.

After 1860, Whipple seems to have drifted away from literary criticism, and set up for a seer in general practice, producing such works as *Character and Characteristic Men.* Only in 1876 does he reappear as critic, in a centennial survey of American literature. It is bad. Here and there a page shows traces of the old Whipple. There are some good observations on Franklin and on the Knickbocker School. But in the main it is hopeless. An enormously disproportionate space is given to orators and theologians. Mark Twain has half a page; William Ellery Channing has five. There is no attempt at discrimination; the later pages are little more than a catalogue of men who had written books in the United States.

If one compares Whipple's essay on Macaulay, published in 1843, with Lowell's first volume, the *Conversations on Some of the Old Poets* (1844), Whipple appears far better as stylist and as thinker. But if one puts Whipple's *Literature and Life* of 1888 beside Lowell's *Old English Dramatists* of the same year, Whipple is nowhere.

CRITICAL WRITINGS OF
E. P. WHIPPLE
PUBLISHED IN BOOK FORM

Essays and Reviews 2 vols.	Appleton, New York, 1848.
Literature and Life	First published in 1849, republished by Houghton Mifflin, Boston, 1888
Literature of the Age of Elizabeth	Fields, Osgood and Co., Boston, 1869
American Literature and Other Papers	Ticknor and Co., Boston, 1887

CHAPTER II

LOWELL

I

ALTHOUGH James Russell Lowell lived on to 1891, and although his best critical work was done after 1865, yet because of his early connection with the *North American*, and because of his many critical connections with the group we have been treating in the last chapter, this seems the logical place to consider him.

Lowell's introduction to criticism did not come through the pages of the *North American*. In 1842, he and Robert Carter founded a magazine called *The Pioneer*. It was the child of youth and hope. Lowell, looking around his native province of Massachusetts, found it a cultural desert, and set out to preach the gospel of culture to a race of benighted materialists. The preface to the first number of *The Pioneer* is filled with this crusading spirit. Lowell begins, like Tudor, by deploring

American dependence on English cultural ideas. What he planned to do was to set up an organ of independent, national criticism, that would assist in bringing forth a new and national literature. He calls, like Tudor twenty-five years before, for a literature to reflect "not only the mountain and the rock, but also the steamboat and the railcar, the cornfield and the factory"; he calls, that is, for realism.

There are two main characteristics evident in this earliest criticism of Lowell's. The first was his desire to evangelize the American public for the sacred cause of literature. For spreading this gospel, Lowell was well fitted. He was well-read in the older poets, he possessed an overflowing enthusiasm for literature, and a capacity for giving that enthusiasm eloquent expression. In the two critical essays he wrote for *The Pioneer* before that magazine's early death, essays on the plays of Middleton and on *Song Writing*, the heart of each essay consists of tactful selections, accompanied by an enthusiastic and appreciative running comment. One might note here that one of Lowell's favorite critical devices, throughout his career, was this method of apt quotation. In the Middleton essay he shows rather higher critical power in his ability to pick out slight but significant indications of character in the plays.

Lowell's theory of poetry at this time was of the sort to inspire him in carrying out his Messianic function. He was a poet before he was a critic; his criticism of this period is the criticism of a young poet, marked by the poet's usual exaggeration of the virtues of his art. He was a firm believer in the Shelleyan, mystical-prophetical view of poetry. "In the poet's lofty heart," he exclaims, "Truth hangs her aery, and thence Love flowers, scattering thence her winged seeds over all the earth with every wind of heaven." "Poets are the forerunners and prophets of changes in the moral world." Echoing the moral view of literature which we have found so pervasive in early American critics, yet echoing it with a significant difference he lays down this law: "The true way of judging the value of any one of the arts is by measuring its aptness and power to advance the refinement and sustain the natural dignity of mankind." The style in which these ideas are expressed fits the thought. It abounds in figures of speech, averaging about three to a sentence, and in capitalized abstractions. It is the prose of a young poet.[1]

[1] Lowell's well-known comment on his own early poetry, in *The Fable for Critics* applies equally well to his early criticism. It is one of the keenest bits of self-criticism in literature.

After the publication of its second number, *The Pioneer* died. When Lowell reappeared as a critic, in 1844, with the *Conversations on some of the Old Poets,* he had grown. He was still the preacher of culture. He was still following closely the early Romantic critics of England. Of American critics, he shows notably the influence of Dana, particularly in his attitude toward Pope. He denies Pope the title of poet, attacks him for his realism, for his verbiage, and compares him unfavorably with the more "natural" Elizabethans.

But in the main the volume is an excellent piece of pioneering. We have seen, in the previous chapter, in what repute Chaucer and Keats were held in America during the thirties. With charming inconsistency, Lowell turns from his attack on the realism of Pope to praise the minute and loving miniatures of real life in Chaucer, although the thing that draws him most to Chaucer is, I think, the old poet's age and remoteness. And of Keats he says that the *Ode to a Nightingale* is the best ode in the English language.

Lowell, like Whipple and Poe, was early conscious of criticism as an art. Scattered through this volume we find his earliest recorded opinions on the art of criticism and on his practice of it. He confesses his bias. "Whenever I love, my delight mounts to an extravagance." "The only safe method is, to point out what parts of a poem please the critic, and let the rest go." He praises the faculty of taste as "the first great requisite of a critic." "We can never say why we love, but only that we love. When we are in the right, we can never reason, but only assert." He makes here, then, no pretence of a judicial attitude, thus repudiating the Eighteenth Century and all its works. His function is to like and to praise, with no other standard than his own critical taste. From this method of pure impressionism he later diverged to some extent; nevertheless, I think that this was essentially his critical procedure throughout his life.

II

Turning temporarily from the Old Poets, Lowell was engaged for the next four years in writing reviews, mainly for the *North American*. Now the reviewing of a current book is an altogether different problem from the appreciation of a classic. It demands a different mode of thought, a different style of expression. It must be the statement of a definite judgment, not the acceptance of one already consecrated by time and authority; it must at least pretend to work from general laws to particular application; it must follow a line of reasoning; and it must be expressed in the prose of reason. But all these things are just what the earlier essays of Lowell lacked. The reviews of the next four years were Lowell's school of criticism.

The first and most famous of these reviews is the *Graham's Magazine* article on Poe. This article is, I think, the chief cause of the disrepute into which Lowell has fallen with certain present-day critics; not, it seems to me, an adequate cause. Lowell begins with a consideration of Poe's verse, to which he gives unreserved praise for its melody, its finish, and its lack of Byronic sentimentalism, then all the rage in American poetry. Stating at once that Poe has genius—and Lowell was not given to lavishing empty compliments on contemporaries—he attempts to pick out the specific qualities of that genius. He finds two; "a faculty of vigorous yet minute analysis, and a wonderful fecundity of imagination." He notes the extreme technical skill and the coldly analytic way in which Poe constructs his emotionally effective tales. Selecting, with the acumen of the born critic, *The Fall of the House of Usher* for particular remark, he says of it, "Had its author written nothing else, it would alone have been sufficient to stamp him as a man of genius, and the master of a classical style." In his praise there are necessarily reservations. With Poe's subject matter, Lowell finds some fault, holding his unreal world to be, not so much a positive defect as a limitation. Finally, he sums the whole matter up in a sentence: "We cannot call his materials the noblest or purest, but we must concede to him the highest merit of construction."

Further evidence of Lowell's early ability to discriminate among contemporary authors is plentiful. Longfellow was the fair-haired child of the *North American.* And yet, writing in that very magazine of Longfellow's prose tale, *Kavanaugh,* Lowell, rather cleverly, very smoothly, but none the less mercilessly concludes that Longfellow is an excellent *poet.* He condemns, with humor and justice, the society novels of D'Israeli and Bulwer. In 1848, he has the vision to say of Browning: "He appears to have a wider range and greater freedom of movement than any other of the younger English poets."

At the end of this four-year period stands the *Fable for Critics,* which is at once a literary credo and a set of rhymed reviews. This is by no means a perfect work of art. There is in it a great deal of pure nonsense, a considerable amount of rather cheap humor, flashes of personal spite and pure malice, notably in the handling of Poe and of Margaret Fuller. But above all these there is a great deal of pure critical genius. There, in words so quotable that they have been quoted to excess, are sketched Bryant's ice-bound reserve, Emerson's queer mixture of mysticism and Yankee horse-sense, Whittier's lyric emotion that fails to find perfect form, Irving's geniality and polish. No other single piece of literary criticism written in America contains so many literary judgments that posterity has accepted as true and orthodox teaching.

During the nine years following, from 1848 to 1857, Lowell did but little critical writing. The decade was spent in writing political articles, in foreign travel, in study abroad, and finally in teaching at Harvard. This period of comparative silence was also a period of great growth, and the first important piece of criticism by which the silence was broken was a masterpiece. This was the introduction to the poems of Keats, written in 1854 and republished in *Among My Books*. In this we find a notable change in critical ideas. The critic who had begun by rhapsodizing about "the poet's lofty heart" now praised Keats chiefly because he "rediscovered the delight and wonder that lay enchanted in the dictionary." This may seem trivial, but it symbolizes a considerable change in Lowell's critical position. He was rapidly growing away from the extreme Romanticism of his earlier years; growing away, too, from his exaggerated notions of the virtues of literature. And as his thinking hardened, his form changed with it. In this essay, almost alone among Lowell's longer critical pieces, there is a definiteness of structure, a sobering down of language. But a short quotation will demonstrate, better than any number of descriptive phrases, the change that was taking place.

> Wordsworth was the deepest thinker, Keats the most essentially a poet, and Byron the most keenly intellectual of the three. Keats had the broadest mind, or at least his mind was open on more sides, and he was able to understand Wordsworth and judge Byron, equally conscious, through his artistic sense, of the greatnesses of the one and the many littlenesses of the other; while Wordsworth was isolated in a feeling of his prophetic character, and Byron had only an uneasy and jealous instinct of contemporary merit.

III

With this essay, Lowell definitely attained critical maturity.[2] Four volumes, *Among My Books*, First

[2] In 1857, Lowell founded the *Atlantic Monthly* as an organ of protest against the conservatism of the *North American Review*. In 1864 he became editor of the *North American*.

Series, (1870), *My Study Windows,* (1871), *Among My Books,* Second Series, (1876), and *Latest Literary Essays and Addresses* (1892), contain the flower of his mature work. These four volumes are pretty much of a piece in critical method, and in literary ideas. Since they are generally conceded to be the most important volumes of literary criticism yet published in America, they deserve an extended examination.

In the field of critical doctrine, we find that Lowell had moved far from the pure impressionism advocated in his earliest work. He now declared that "To look at all sides, and to distrust the verdict of a single mood, is, no doubt, the duty of a critic." He reasserted this, coupled with the statement that there are fixed principles of art on which criticism can be based, in his longest pronouncement on critical theory.

I have often thought that, unless we can so far free ourselves from our prepossessions, as to be capable of bringing to a work of art some freshness of sensation, and receiving from it in turn some new surprise of sympathy and admiration—some shock, even, it may be, of instinctive dislike and repulsion—though we may praise or blame, weighing our pros and cons in the nicest balances, sealed by the proper authority, yet we shall not criticize in the highest sense. On the other hand, unless we admit certain principles as fixed beyond question, we shall be able to render no adequate judgment, but only to record our impressions.

Again he says, reverting almost to the Eighteenth Century, "Criticism is the unbiased application of certain well-defined and self-existent principles of judgment."

Here we have two antithetical systems of criticism in head-on collision. It is like attempting to cross the ideas of Walter Pater with those of Taine; and not all of Professor Foerster's logic can resolve them into a higher synthesis.

Lowell had, then, a philosophy of literature. To recover that philosophy from the pages of his criticism is no easy matter, and one must at times take the long chance of putting words into his mouth. At times, literature appears to Lowell as an escape. For all of his apparent worldly success, for all his capacity for friendship, there was yet a shy and elusive quality in Lowell's nature, a super-sensitive idealism that shrank from stark reality and found in literature a refuge from life. "Give me," he cries, "the writers who take me for awhile out of myself and away from my neighbors." He speaks of imaginative literature as "the realm of might-be, our haven of refuge from the short-comings and disillusions of life." As early as in his lectures of 1855 we find this desire for escape, and it crops up at intervals all through his writings.

It follows naturally from this outlook on literature that the type of writing to which Lowell turned, in his search for a refuge, was not the essay, which is the reflection of a literary mind over its actual experiences, nor the novel, which in its highest form always approaches as closely as possible to the facts of real life, but what he felicitously calls "the other-world of poetry." Every one of Lowell's greatest and most appreciative essays deals with a poet, usually the poet of some remote and distance-mellowed age. Chaucer, Shakespeare, Dante, Spenser, Dryden, Pope—these are the subjects of his best work. There is nowhere a finer glorification of this aspect of literature than the essay on Spenser.

In this respect, then, Lowell remained a Romanticist. Indeed, much that he had learned from the early romantic critics he retained through life. As late as the Chaucer essay of 1870 we find him reverting to the notion of the poet as prophet and seer. "Poems," he there says, "are not made of words and thoughts and images, but of that something in the poet himself which can compel them to obey him and move to the rhythm of his nature."

From the romantic critics also Lowell learned to talk much about the Imagination. He even finds it necessary to set up the old antithesis of Fancy and Imagination, and to attempt a differentiation between those elusive categories.

Lowell's position in regard to realism is not easy to make out. He shifted and veered, not only between youth and maturity, but at various points within his mature period. In general, we may regard him as an anti-realist, his view summed up in the following dictum: "I confess that in the productions of what is called the realistic school I too often find myself in company that is little to my taste, dragged back into a commonplace world from which I was only too glad to escape." Zola he viewed as the type of modern realism, and several times went out of his way to make disparaging asides about that author. It is curious and entertaining to note his attitude toward Fielding. The voice of posterity had declared Fielding a classic, and Lowell did not easily dispute the voice of posterity. He seems to feel under obligation to praise Fielding, but there is in that praise a note of reserve that contrasts sharply with his bursts of enthusiasm over the authors he really liked. Yet he had too catholic a taste to be entirely deaf to realism. Thus we find him remarking, in the course of a discussion on the pre-Shakespearian rhymed tragedies, "*Gammer Gurton's Needle* is worth the whole of them. It may be coarse, earthy, but in reading it one feels that he is at least a man among men, and not a humbug among humbugs." And for a man of Lowell's critical tastes and critical ancestry, his judgment of Pope is one of the rare instances in the history of criticism of true detachment. Accepting neither the doctrine prevalent in this country well into the Nineteenth Century, that Pope was the true father of English poetry, nor his own early judgment that Pope was no poet at all, Lowell arrives at a genuinely independent and sound view of the poet, finding the excellence of his work to consist in the fact that his poetry "was a mirror in a drawing-room, but it gave you back a faithful image of a society, powdered and rouged to be sure, and intent on trifles, yet still as human in its way as the heroes of Homer in theirs."

All these are Romantic elements. But in one important respect Lowell was far from being a romanticist—was indeed, throughout his mature life in revolt against romanticism. He had begun as a Utopian reformer; that is, as a sentimentalist. Outgrowing this, like many converts he conceived a bitter dislike for his older faith, and endeavored with all his powers to smash the idol of his earlier worship. Beginning with the essay on Wordsworth in 1854, he devoted a large part of his criticism through the years 1854–1870 to a smashing attack on sentimentalism. He considers the Wordsworthian view of nature as a consoler and a refuge an unhealthy and unnatural piece of sentimentalism. "Those," he says, "who have most loudly advertised their passion for solitude and their intimacy with Nature, from Petrarch down, have been mostly sentimentalists." For the same reason he condemns Thoreau.

Another form of sentimentalism, an even worse form, Lowell thought, was the modern tendency toward individualism and introspection. He had no use for "that exaggeration of the individual, and depression of the social man, which has become the cant of modern literature." Such a cult was fatal to great poetry. "The artist period," he insisted, "begins precisely at the point where the pleasure of expressing self ends, and the poet becomes sensible that his highest duty is to give voice to the myriad forms of nature, which wanting him were dumb. . . . Hence Shakespeare, the truest of artists, is nothing more than a voice." He complained that

"Latterly, poetry seems to have deserted the strong and palpable motions of the common heart, and to have devoted itself to the ecstatic exploration of solitary nerves—the less tangible, the better."

As an anti-sentimentalist, Lowell attacked Dickens, crying out against "that melodramatic sentimentality with which Dickens infected so much of the literature of the day." Carlyle came up for judgment next, and although the essay as a whole is favorable to Carlyle, nearly a third is devoted to a sound tongue-lashing of the burly Scotchman for his sentimentality, with its corollaries, egotism, cynicism, wrongheaded dogmatism, and sensationalism. But the completest expression of this anti-sentimental crusade is contained in the long article of 1867, *Rousseau and the Sentimentalists*. Here is a bitter attack on the whole tribe of sentimentalists: Burke and Ruskin, because they mistook "their own personal likes and dislikes, tastes and distastes, for general principles"; Chateaubriand and Lamartine, the "lackeys of fine phrases"; all the professed nature-worshippers from Petrarch down, but with Wordsworth now excepted; all the writers of posing autobiographies and confessions, St. Augustine included; and finally Rousseau, whom Lowell considered "the highest type of the sentimentalist of genius." With this essay, Lowell seems to have achieved a sort of catharsis, and sentimentalism troubled him but little more.

This essay adds but little to Lowell's stature as a critic. It is an attack, and Lowell was never at his best when attacking. But it does affect one's estimate of Lowell as a man—this passionate crusade against insincerity, which goes far to prove how genuine was Lowell's love of reserve, manliness, truth. Yet I wonder if the bitterness of the attack was not due largely to Lowell's unconscious feeling that he himself had been, perhaps to some extent still was, a sentimentalist. I suspect he has given us the key himself in this same essay, where, speaking of Burke's hatred of Rousseau, he remarks, "It was so genuine and so instinctive as no hatred can be but that of self, of our weaknesses as we see them in another." Such candor, carried almost to the point of naïveté, is rather common in Lowell, and one of his most engaging characteristics.

Turning away definitely, then, both from romanticism and from realism, Lowell, in his search for a literary creed to which he might subscribe arrived eventually at a sort of classicism. Thus he reiterated again and again the doctrine, which may ultimately be traced back to Aristotle, that literature should not consist of purple patches. The great quality of the great writers is their imagination, which Lowell defined as "the shaping quality." Possessed of this quality, it is the function of the great poets to "exalt men's minds, and give a right direction and safe outlet to their passions through the imagination, while insensibly helping them toward balance of character and serenity of judgment by stimulating their sense of proportion, form, and the nice adjustment of means to ends."

Nowhere can this classic element of Lowell's thought be better studied than in the Dryden essay of 1868. In accordance with one of his earliest principles of criticism, Lowell here attempts to get behind previous judgments of Dryden, and to see the man afresh. Thus he states his purpose: "It is perhaps worth while to take a fresh observation of him, to consider him neither as warning nor example, but to make out what it is that has given so lofty and firm a position to one of the most unequal, inconsistent, and faulty writers that ever lived." But note that Lowell does not question Dryden's position in the histories. He accepts that position as finally settled by the general voice of criticism, and endeavors only to discover the basis for that accepted judgment. Lowell finds the excellence of Dryden to consist in just those qualities which the romantic critics, and Lowell in his earlier days, would have condemned; he praises Dryden for the logical structure of his prose, for his ability to reason in verse, above all for the hearty, common-sense masculinity of his character. Finally the critic lets himself go in a passage of genuine critical eloquence.

> Amid the rickety sentiment looming big through misty phrase which marks so much of modern literature, to read him is as bracing as a northeast wind. He blows the mind clear.

Not only is this essay classical in its critical thought. It is one of the few in which Lowell reached something like classical form. It is constructed, not thrown together, free from digressions, comparatively plain in style, subdued in its figures of speech. It is not Lowell at his most characteristic, nor even Lowell at his point of highest flight; it is, perhaps, Lowell at his rounded best.

Closely allied with this Greek insistence on form and proportion is Lowell's doctrine of the social nature of great literature. "The greatest poets," he remarks, with a glance aside at Wordsworth and Thoreau, "I think, have found man more interesting than nature." More sweepingly he asserts, "I cannot recall that isolation has produced anything in literature better than monkish chronicles." The poėt's function he considered primarily social. The great poet is no longer the prophet of changes in the moral world; all great artistic minds are primarily conservative. The poet should be one "singing amid the throngs of men, and lifting their common aspirations and sympathies with wings of his song to a purer ether and a wider reach of view."

It will be noted that not only does the quotation which announced Lowell's conversion to classicism contain a classical view of art: it also implies a moral—perhaps I had better call it an ethical—view. And thus, by way of romanticism, anti-sentimentalism, and finally classicism, Lowell came back to the moral in literature. But this was no mere reversion to the Puritanism of the *North American* fathers. Lowell insists, as fervently as Poe, that literature is not a sermon. But form, balance, reserve, masculinity—these are moral, as well as literary qualities, and Lowell does not believe that they can be exhibited in great literature without a moral effect. This is, of course, in complete contradiction to Lowell's notion and use of literature as an escape from life. This contradiction he never resolved.

Thus we find him at one time stating that "genius is not a question of character"; again that "every man feels instinctively that all the beautiful sentiments in the world weigh less than a single lovely action." Particularly in the Spenser essay this contradiction appears. I give below two sentences which contain these two notions, and leave the reader to judge which is the more sincere, the better Lowell, and the better criticism.

> No man can read the "Faerie Queene" and be anything but the better for it.
>
> Whoever can endure unmixed delight, whoever can tolerate music and painting and poetry all in one, whoever wishes to be rid of thought and to let the busy anvils of the brain be silent for a time, let him read in the "Faerie Queene." There is the land of pure heart's ease, where no ache nor sorrow of spirit can enter.

These, then, are the elements of Lowell's philosophy of literature—a philosophy by no means complete and harmonious. Professor Foerster has recently, with considerable ingenuity, gathered these scattered ideas and dicta into a sort of Lowellian critical creed. This process, while cleverly carried out, does not, I think, fairly represent Lowell. It was one of Lowell's characteristics not to be consistent, not to organize his doctrines into a summa.

These ideas do not fit together, and they can only be made to appear to do so by a process of rationalization that was far indeed from Lowell's mind.[3]

IV

So much for Lowell's theory; now for his practice. One of the first things to be noted about that practice is the nature of his subjects. We have seen Lowell in his early days as an alert and sympathetic critic of contemporary literature. But in his later years, turning away as he did from both romanticism and realism, he naturally found himself out of sympathy with practically all of the literature of his day. His farewell to modern literature, to all intents and purposes, was the Percival essay of 1866—and it is noteworthy that this was the only purely destructive piece of criticism he ever attempted. It is good in its line—fully as devastating as Macaulay's famous attack on Montgomery and far more good-humored. But Lowell was not at his best in attack, as I think he realized, and with this article, his consideration of modern literature ends. We have then the interesting spectacle of a critic

[3] Foerster's exaggeration is in part, I think, a reaction from the opposite extreme, expressed most fully by Reilly, that Lowell had no doctrines, only tastes. This view Foerster has completely and finally demolished.

of high rank, living in the midst of a highly productive period, and paying apparently not the slightest attention to the productions of that period. Eliot, Rossetti, Morris, Meredith, Hardy, Pater, Stevenson—one might think he had never heard their names. He even ceased to take any apparent interest in American literature. Men with whom he must have been personally acquainted—men with whom we know him to have been closely associated, were forgotten when he came to write. One might expect him to pass by Whitman, but it is rather startling to find no mention in his later pages of Howells or James or Aldrich or Mark Twain.

Some men are born reviewers; Lowell had the ability, but not the taste. One can almost hear the sigh of relief with which he turned at last from the consideration of contemporaries, and ended, as he had begun, with the Old Poets. He celebrated this holiday by throwing off the limitations of the review in form and space. As magazine articles, his essays became mastodonic. The review of Hazlitt's *Library of Old Authors* occupies a large part of two issues of the *North American.* He no longer needed to compress nor bothered to construct. The first of his longer essays were fairly well-built; later they became rambling, diffuse, merely thrown together. This change was partly due to the feeling of luxurious licentiousness which his established position brought with it, partly to innate lack of constructive power, partly to pure mental laziness. But it is also true that like the mature Shakespeare, he now had more to say than the form in which he was working would contain. He was a man past middle age, who had read much, seen much, felt much, even thought much, in scraps and flashes. When he took up the pen, more ideas ran to his head than he could manage, and he lacked the intellectual power to select and reject. Every idea suggested another, and he put them all down. Such essays as the *Chaucer* and the *Dante* are not merely essays on Chaucer and Dante; they are mines of mediæval scholarship.

The essay on Chaucer shows Lowell at his most characteristic. It begins with a statement of Chaucer's general qualities, with a pen picture of his appearance. Then follows an aside of two pages on Sir Harris Nicholas's life of Chaucer, discussing the question of Chaucer's possible complicity in the insurrection of John of Northampton. After this we have a section of twenty pages on Chaucer's literary predecessors—the Troubadours, the Trouvères, and the Anglo-Saxon poets. Then comes a comparison of Chaucer and Dante, and a brief discussion of Gower and Langland. The fourteen pages following contain a lengthy and minute study of Chaucer's prosody. The essay concludes with a general appreciation of Chaucer, and a placing of him in the history of English poetry.

And even this does not show Lowell at his most discursive point. The *Library of Old Authors* breaks into three almost unrelated sections, an appreciation of the Elizabethan dramatists, a dissertation on philology, and an essay on translating Homer. But *Shakespeare Once More* is the prize specimen. It sounds, in summary, like a cross-section of a literary encyclopedia.

I emphasize this tendency to ramble because it seems to me highly indicative of a mental weakness. Fine as these larger essays are, there is in them a perceptible relaxing of mental fibre. In the first of the major essays, those on Wordsworth, Dryden, Carlyle, Rousseau, there was a definite intellectual approach to the subject. In them, Lowell formulates and makes use of his laws of literature, though not with thorough consistency. In the Wordsworth piece, for example, after trying Wordsworth by his own canons and finding him wanting, Lowell hedges in the end, and accepts Wordsworth's position in English poetry as Arnold had earlier fixed it. But in these later works, judicial criticism is definitely abandoned. Dealing with men whose position had long been as fixed in literary history as the stars in heaven, he was under no necessity of placing. He could give himself up, solely and completely, to the luxury of admiration.

And this brings us to the one thing in criticism that Lowell could do supremely well. With Lowell, the significant and memorable part of his criticism is the summing up, the general descriptive sentences that one finds at the beginning and end of his essays. He has a positive genius for giving fresh and eloquent expression to orthodox literary opinion. He accepts orthodoxy in literature, but in no blind or half-hearted manner. He has all the enthusiasm for Dante that faddist critics discover for Mallarmé, or Ambrose Bierce, or Arthur Machen. I know of no finer passage, in the whole realm of "books about books," than the beginning of the Chaucer essay. It abounds with quotable sentences.

There is a prevading wholesomeness in the writings of this man—a vernal property that soothes and refreshes in a way of which no other has ever found the secret.

It is good to retreat now and then beyond earshot of

the introspective confidences of modern literature, and to lose ourselves in the gracious worldliness of Chaucer.

One feels, in these passages and many another like them, the freshness of the classic—and also the freshness of Lowell. And this comes, note, from no application of the immutable "laws of literature." It is the product of that same instinctive ear for the best in literature that led Lowell to single out Bryant and Emerson and Poe from the crowd of poetasters who surrounded them and often obscured them in the eyes of less discerning critics.

This special quality of singling out the best in literature, and for writing, with contagious enthusiasm, one's appreciation of that best, was of particular service in the American criticism of the early Nineteenth Century; one quality of that criticism being its sad lack of perspective, so that Barlow was hailed as an epic genius, and Miss Huntly's *Moral Pieces* were thought "sublime."

V

At the very end of Lowell's career stand two volumes, *Latest Literary Essays and Addresses,* and *The Old English Dramatists,* which for several reasons demand separate consideration. For ten years, from 1876 to 1886, Lowell kept silence. In the latter year was published the first of the studies collected in these volumes, the essay on Gray.

This essay opens with a general discussion of the Eighteenth Century. After admitting that "a certain blight of propriety seems to have fallen on the verse of that age," Lowell confesses that "as one grows older, one finds more points of half-reluctant sympathy with that undyspeptic and rather worldly period, much in the same way as one grows to find a keener savor in Horace and Montaigne." He gives free reign to his growing conservatism, praising the American Revolution as an essentially reactionary step in history, wistfully admiring the Eighteenth Century doctrine of human perfectibility, envying the possibility of seclusion for the scholar of that day. He then proceeds to list, with an appropriate word for each, the great men produced by that century.

All this sounds like a typical Lowell meander; it is, as a matter of fact, closely related to the criticism of Gray. Lowell now proceeds to show that to some extent both the excellences and the deficiencies of Gray as a poet were the results of the contact of his peculiar mind with the temper of his age. In this, of course, he is in agreement with Arnold's famous article. But his final conclusion is diametrically the opposite of Arnold's. Arnold makes out Gray's failure to produce more and greater poetry the result of his disharmony with his age—"he was a poet in an age of prose." Lowell finds the cause rather in Gray's own temperament—or, to put it more plainly, his laziness.[4]

Finally, in 1892, Lowell closed the long circle of his criticism by a return to some of the subjects of his earliest volume. In this last production, *The Old English Dramatists,* written when he was sixty-eight years old, the veteran collected his final opinions on life and literature. An interesting contrast exists between these essays and those of his central period. There is a return here to the judicial method, which Lowell had used in his treatment of Wordsworth and Carlyle. There is here also a refreshing independence of tradition. All through the Nineteenth Century, critics were saying over and over again the Lamb-Hazlitt-Swinburne doctrine, that the Elizabethans were all giants and demigods. Lowell himself, in his earliest volume, had confessed to this faith. But now, secure in his clas-

[4] There is an interesting question of dates here. Lowell's essay sounds like an answer to Arnold. The dates of publication make this possible. Arnold's essay was published in 1880, Lowell's in 1886. But Norton states that Lowell's *Gray* was largely written by 1870.

sicism, he turns away from critical orthodoxy, and anticipates by thirty years William Archer and the moderns. He boldly calls Greene dull and inadequate; says that we can get along very well without Peele; and disparages Webster, Beaumont and Fletcher, and even Marlowe. His final word on the whole group is that they "are the best comment to convince us of the immeasurable superiority of Shakespeare."

This is perhaps carrying classicism to an excess. We can hardly agree when Lowell finds that Marlowe has no central purpose or organic unity, though there is, as Lowell points out, a long step between Marlowe's "fine madness" and "the imperturbable sanity of Shakespeare." But though particular condemnations may seem excessive, the motive behind them was right. In words that might have been spoken by Sainte-Beuve in one of his most classical moods, Lowell declares that the trouble with the minor Elizabethans is "want of taste, of sense of congruity, and of the delicate discrimination that makes style." And then, demonstrating the proper use of scholarship in literature, he draws a parallel worth quoting.

There is something in Webster that reminds me of Victor Hugo. There is the same confusion at times of what is big with what is great, the same fondness for the merely spectacular, the same insensibility to repulsive details, the same indifference to the probable or even the natural, the same leaning toward the grotesque, the same love of effect at whatever cost; and there is also the same impressiveness of result.

Of all the writers of the period, Lowell picks out for his particular approval the rather neglected figure of Philip Massinger.[5] Finding in Massinger that desirable quality of manliness, he grows enthusiastic over "the love he shows for those things that are lovely and of good report in human nature, for his sympathy with what is generous and high-minded and honorable, and his equable flow of a good, everyday kind of poetry with few rapids or cataracts, but singularly soothing and companionable."

There are many points in this volume on which one might dilate—the recurrence of the escape motif, the sober charm of the style, the total lack of most of Lowell's irritating tricks and mannerisms. But I cannot forbear quoting Lowell's final definition of poetry—a definition set up in opposition to Arnold. "Poetry is a criticism of life only in the

[5] It is an interesting confirmation of Lowell's judgment that Massinger stood the test of stage performance longer than any other Elizabethan outside of Shakespeare.

sense that it furnishes us with the standard of a more ideal felicity, of calmer pleasures and more majestic pains." Whether one agrees with that or not, whether one agrees with the specific judgments of this volume, one cannot escape the fact that it shows a man near seventy and still growing. In independence of mind, in pure thinking power, in control over form and style, in sanity and balance, this last volume is Lowell's best work.

VI

To place Lowell in his proper station in the order of American critics is no easy task. In fact, such a placement depends so wholly on one's notion of what criticism ought to be, that it can never be done with general satisfaction. On the one hand we have Professor Woodberry informing us that Lowell "is the only critic of high rank that our literature owns." On the other hand, the author of the most extensive study of Lowell's criticism, Dr. Reilly, concludes that he is not a critic at all. And Mr. Mencken abruptly dismisses him as a "snob." There is a passage in one of Lowell's own essays that gets very near to the heart of the matter. Lowell is speaking of Thoreau.

> His appreciation is of the highest quality; his critical power, from want of continuity of mind, very limited and inadequate. . . . He had none of the artistic mastery which controls a great work to completeness, but exquisite mechanical skill in the shaping of sentences or paragraphs.

There is Lowell in his own looking-glass.

But regardless of one's own estimate of Lowell, there is no question that he was, during the last half of the Nineteenth Century, universally accepted as the greatest American critic of literature. Standing in a position almost comparable to that of Dr. Johnson, his influence was deep and pervading. From his work flowed three main critical currents.

First, there were the direct imitators, the men who, observing how closely Lowell kept his eye on the greatest writers, devoted their energies to long essays, appreciative in character, on the major classics. The best of this group was Professor Woodberry; the worst, Hamilton Wright Mabie, who managed to be something like a Lowell in malicious caricature.

Far more important than any influence through these obvious followers was the tremendous impulse Lowell gave to literary scholarship in America. Begun by Ticknor, advanced by Longfellow, it was to Lowell that the growth of interest in mediæval and

Elizabethan literature was mainly due. The study of English in our universities has even reflected his particular bent towards Chaucer and Dante. Norton, Kittredge, Wright, Cook, Manly, Gayley—in some sense Lowell is the literary father of all these men, whose collective influence on literary thought in this country has been immeasurable.

A third stream of literary thought has flowed from Lowell. From Lowell's *Rousseau and the Sentimentalists* to Professor Babbitt's *Rousseau and Romanticism* is but a short step; and thus, through his attack on Romanticism—or at least on some sides of Romanticism—and his emphasis on classic virtues, Lowell became the teacher of the present-day Humanist school of American critics.

BIBLIOGRAPHY

Lowell's more important critical works, arranged in chronological order. Titles in italics are those of bound volumes.

The standard edition of Lowell is that published by Houghton Mifflin. All articles starred are to be found in this edition.

The Old English Dramatists	Boston Miscellany, April, May, August, 1842
Plays of Middleton *	Pioneer, February, 1843

LOWELL

Song Writing *	Pioneer, February, 1843
Conversations on Some of the Old Poets	Cambridge, 1844
Edgar Allan Poe *	Graham's Magazine, February, 1845
The New Timon Among the Poets	North American Review, April, 1847
Browning's Plays and Poems	North American Review, April, 1848
A Fable for Critics	New York, 1848
Introduction to *Keat's Poems* *	Boston, 1854
Introduction to *Wordsworth's Poems* *	Boston, 1854
Library of Old Authors *	Atlantic Monthly, April, May, 1858
White's Shakespeare	Atlantic Monthly, January, February, 1859
Thoreau *	North American Review, October, 1865
Swinburne's Tragedies *	North American Review, April, 1866
Carlyle *	North American Review, October, 1866
Rousseau and the Sentimentalists *	North American Review, July, 1867
Shakespeare Once More *	North American Review, April, 1868

Dryden *	North American Review, July, 1868
Chaucer *	Appleton's *New American Encyclopedia*
Among My Books, First Series	Boston, 1870
Pope *	North American Review, April, 1871
My Study Windows	Boston, 1871
Masson's Life of Milton *	North American Review, January, 1872
Spenser *	North American Review, April, 1875
Walton *	Nation, April 27, 1876
Among My Books, Second Series	Boston, 1876
Gray *	New Princeton Review, March, 1886
Letters of Walter Savage Landor *	Century, February, 1888
Shakespeare's Richard III *	Atlantic Monthly, December, 1891
Latest Literary Essays and Addresses	Boston, 1892
Marlowe *	Harper, July, 1892
Webster *	Harper, August, 1892
Chapman *	Harper, September, 1892
Beaumont and Fletcher *	Harper, October, 1892
Massinger and Ford *	Harper, November, 1892
The Old English Dramatists	Boston, 1892

LOWELL

STUDIES OF LOWELL'S CRITICISM

Robertson, J. M., *Lowell as a Critic,* North Am. Rev., June, 1919

Macy, John, *The Spirit of American Literature,* Garden City, Doubleday, Page, 1913. Republished in The Modern Library, Boni & Liveright.

Reilly, J. J., *James Russell Lowell as a Critic,* New York, Putnam, 1915.

Woodberry, George E., *Makers of Literature,* New York, Macmillan, 1900.

Brownell, W. C., *American Prose Masters,* Scribner, New York, 1909.

Foerster, Norman, *American Criticism,* Houghton Mifflin, Boston, 1928.

CHAPTER III

Poe

I

In 1845 the editor of *Graham's Magazine* asked James Russell Lowell, then a clever young critic from Boston, to review certain prose tales recently published by a new writer from Virginia, Edgar Allan Poe. Thus came together for the first time the two greatest American literary critics of the day, the representatives of two streams of literary tendency in America.

There is a singular contrast between the two men. Lowell, the favorite son of the New England Brahmins, professor at Harvard, ambassador to England, lived on until 1891, becoming the nearest to a literary dictator we have yet had. Poe, outcast and erratic, after struggling for a few years to make a bare living, died in the gutter, and was buried beneath a heap of Pharasaic censure. Like the fates of the two men have been the fates of their critical writings. Lowell has been the most widely accepted of American critics, but no two men seem able to agree as to the merits of Poe's criticism. Opinions have ranged all the way from the supercilious sneer of Henry James—that it is "probably the most complete and exquisite specimen of provincialism ever prepared for the edification of men"—to Robertson's sweeping statement that it "will better stand critical examination today than any similar work produced in America or England in his time." Until twenty years ago, James's view was rather generally received, but now literary fashions have changed, and it is in vogue to sneer at Lowell and to laud Poe. Amid this welter of opinions one fact stands out clearly: Lowell is read. His phrases have passed into our histories of literature. His books are still in print. As for Poe, three essays, *The Poetic Principle, The Rationale of Verse,* and *The Philosophy of Composition,* are well known, but save when disturbed by the occasional prowlings of the special student, the rest of his criticism gathers dust on the library shelves.

A reading of Poe's criticism convinces one of two things; that he has something to say that is genuinely worth saying, and that he is never likely to gain an opportunity of saying it to the general reader.

The reason for this will appear clearly as we go on.

For convenience, Poe's criticism may be divided into two parts; reviews of specific writers, and general discussions of literary theory—metacritic, George Saintsbury would call it. A mere glance at the titles of his reviews reveals at once one of the main reasons why he is unread—and why Lowell is read. By far the larger and more important part of Lowell's criticism deals with great authors—Spenser, Chaucer, Pope, Dryden, Gray. And even when Lowell undertook to review contemporaries, he had an uncanny instinct for picking out the one man in a group of twenty who was destined to survive. Practically every man treated at any length in *A Fable for Critics* is still a living name in the world of literature. Poe, on the contrary, treated every author who came his way, even showing a tendency to select by choice the worse rather than the better. There was an excellent reason for this, but it hurts him now. As a result, Lowell is doubly sure of an audience. His essay on Chaucer is read both by those who are interested in Lowell and by those who are interested in Chaucer. The ordinary reader, to whom literature is a diversion, wants to know what Lowell has to say about the *Faerie Queene*. But he cares very little what Poe has to say about

Moore's *Alciphron* or Seba Smith's *Powhatan.* It is exasperating that so much critical intelligence should have been wasted on the consideration of men not worth the trouble. One ought not to use a sixteen-inch gun to shoot sparrows.

II

Turning first to Poe's reviews, let us look at his critical method. In spite of his pronounced Romantic leanings, his criticism is in at least two important respects in the full Eighteenth Century tradition. It is invariably judicial. Poe had very definite opinions as to the merits of the authors he read, and no hesitancy whatever about expressing those opinions flatly. And these opinions always appear, not as the result of pure inspiration or of innate taste, but as reasoned conclusions from general principles.[1] Does he wish to deny high poetic rank to Drake? He first sets up a distinction between the fancy and the imagination. (All respectable critics of the early Nineteenth Century did this. Poe's distinguishing mark is that he makes sense of it.) On the basis of this distinction he proceeds to show that Drake has only the lesser quality. Does he wish to

[1] All destructive critics make a parade of doing this. But one does not feel that with Poe, as with Lowell, the reason comes after the conclusion.

form a judgment of Hawthorne's tales? He preludes his essay by a definition of the prose tale. Does he wish to condemn the didacticism of Longfellow? He must first limit the respective provinces of truth and beauty in poetry.

No one could say of Poe, as has been so often said of modern reviewers, that he was not in the habit of reading the books he reviewed. Once he had made his definition, stated his general law, established his major premise, he proceeded in logical fashion to prove his case, not by vague generalizations, but by a most minute examination of the books under review. Nothing was too small to escape his critical eye, no detail too trivial, no analysis too technical. Consider, for instance, his article on Longfellow's *Spanish Student*. He begins by discussing the general theme of the play, endeavoring to find out how far Longfellow's conception is original.[2] From the theme, he proceeds logically to the plot. Here his first move is to give a synopsis of the whole story. Then follows a discussion of the relevancy of certain scenes, Poe taking pains in each case to show just why the incident in question adds nothing to the advance of the plot. After this,

[2] This obsession with originality was one of Poe's worst critical defects, due, I think, to his lack of knowledge of literary history, which would have taught him the rarity of originality, even among the greatest.

he points out half a dozen inconsistencies in the conduct of the story. Finally, he shoots the whole plot full of holes by naming incident after incident that is as old as the hills and as stage-worn as the missing will. The plot thus disposed of, Poe attacks Longfellow's attempts at humor—mainly by the simple yet effective device of quotation without comment. Finally, the facts being all presented, he arrives at the conclusion that the whole piece, while containing here and there a line of passable poetry, is as a play quite unworthy of any critical respect.

This attention to detail is highly characteristic of all his criticism. He never discusses poetry without delving into scansion, without noting bad rhymes, misplaced accents. He spends two pages in a review of *Horseshoe Robinson* in calling attention to mistakes in punctuation. He is forever assailing authors for their errors in grammar. Here is a typical bit from a review of Bryant.

> The five concluding lines of the stanza are not equally effective:
>
> When o'er the buds of youth the death-wind blows,
> And blights the fairest; when our bitterest tears
> Stream, as the eyes of those that love us close,
> We think on what they were, with many fears
> Lest goodness die with them, and leave the coming years.

> The defects here, are all of a metrical and of course minor nature, but are still defects. The line:
>
> When o'er the buds of youth the death-wind blows
>
> is impeded in its flow by the final *th* in *youth,* and especially in *death* where *w* follows. The word *tears* cannot readily be pronounced after the final *st* in *bitterest;* and its own final consonant, *rs,* in like manner renders an effort necessary in the utterance of *stream,* which commences the next line.

Now all this makes Poe a good critic, but it also makes him extraordinarily hard reading. He is technical, and rightly so; but that is not all of criticism. It is not even the most pleasant part of criticism. It is, however, a necessary part, especially for the kind of criticism Poe was attempting. The foundation of judicial criticism, if the judgment is to be worth anything, must be an examination of technicalities. Unfortunately the ordinary intelligent reader, to whom literature is an amusement, is not interested in technicalities. A few pages of the sort of thing I have quoted above put him to sleep. And here we have a second reason why Poe stays on the shelf.

III

Max Beerbohm once divided critics into two classes, those who feel and those who think. To the former group Lowell belongs. He had ideas, excellent and sound ideas; but they came in flashes and were never worked into a system. He depends largely, in his criticism, on the exercise and expression of his unusually sound and sure taste. Poe is here again his exact opposite. At first glance, one would unhesitatingly class the author of *The Fall of the House of Usher* and *Annabel Lee* as an emotionalist—and correctly. But when the emotionalist, or even the sensualist, can reason in any sort, he is likely to reason with unequalled power and clearness. Poe himself noted and commented on this frequent and yet surprising combination of faculties. "The reasoning powers," he asserted, "never exist in perfection unless when allied with a high degree of the imaginative faculty." In his tales, his poems, his life, Poe appears to the superficial student as the incarnation of the popular notion of the literary man—a creature of pure feeling, of sensitive, tingling nerves, unordered by reason. In his criticism, we are more often reminded of the man who offered to solve any cipher the readers of his magazine might send him—and who did it.

He is, within his limits, the shrewdest reasoner in the field of literary criticism. Not that he made the Eighteenth Century mistake of applying the test of common sense to everything in literature. He was too good a reasoner for that. He carefully allowed for the function of the emotions in literature; his theory of literature is built on the function of the emotions. But he insisted on treating the emotions logically. He put his whole critical dependence on reasoned conclusions—and thereby fell into error. He had in perfection the art of putting two and two together; but in criticism, unfortunately, two and two do not always make four. They must be stretched to make five, or seven, or sometimes seventeen. A poem may be composed of four lines, but an examination of those four lines with respect to scansion, rhyme scheme, diction, and ideas, no matter how keenly and searchingly carried out, does not quite bring us to a complete and final judgment of the poem. After all the syllables have been counted, after all the ideas have been evaluated, the critic is still a measurable distance from his destination. To bridge the gap, he has nothing on which he can rely save that mysterious quality which we might call the ear for literature. And it is just at this point that Poe most often fails.

One would look far to find a critic of equal rank with an equal number of silly blunders to his discredit. Poe's processes were always admirable, but when it came to the final step, his taste was subject to frequent and ridiculous aberrations. Of contemporary English novelists, he knows of none "that possess the power of Bulwer." He goes even further. "Viewing Bulwer as a novelist," he grandly declares, "he is unsurpassed by any writer living or dead." Southey is "great in every department of literature he has attempted." Tennyson sends him into ecstasies. "In perfect sincerity I regard him as the noblest poet that ever lived." But most marvellous of all his wildcat admirations is his positive idolatry of Moore. Moore "is the most skillful literary artist of his day—perhaps of any day." Of Moore's *Alciphron* he sweepingly remarks, "We could not point out a poem in any language which, as a whole, greatly excels it." [3]

This hysterical admiration for second-rate writers is Poe's greatest fault. It is due, of course, primarily

[3] There was, I suspect, an element of pure contrariness in this attitude toward Moore. We have already noted the disfavor in which Moore was held by the critics of the *North American,* and Poe had no love for the men of that group.

to his lack of training. Lowell, with a scholarship ranging over thirty centuries and six literatures, saw things in proportion and perspective, while Poe, having almost no standards of comparison outside of his contemporaries, was apt to mistake pigmies for giants. Of course, there is another side to the picture. The man who habitually lives with Dante and Chaucer and Spenser is apt to develop a sort of literary snobbishness, to become blind to contemporary excellence; as indeed Lowell did.

Fortunately, Poe was not often in this mood. Most of his specific judgments were correct. He was one of the first critics in America to appreciate Dickens. He saw clearly that Bryant stood far above all the other American poets previous to 1830. He hailed Longstreet's *Georgia Scenes* as a "sure omen of better days for the literature of the South." Four years after it was made, he retracted his first judgment of Bulwer, and placed that gentleman among the second-raters. With exceeding critical tact, he separated the mountain of chaff in Longfellow from the small but precious half-bushel of poetry. And one of the keenest bits of critical analysis in the history of the art is his review of Macaulay's essays. In two pages, he gives us Macaulay in a nutshell—his clarity, his closeness of logic, his practical sagacity and fatal lack of depth, his dazzling luminousness which prevents our seeing the casuistry behind it—all set forth with a keenness and clearness unexcelled by Macaulay himself.

IV

But since Poe was always systematically judicial, his likes, whether right or wrong, were of less importance than his dislikes. Systematic judicial criticism is primarily a means, not of discovering truth, but of exposing error. The particular function of the judicial critic, the thing that he can do and that no one else can do, is the flagellation of bad authors. It is impossible to comprehend or to appreciate Poe's critical work unless one understands clearly that he was a literary reformer. Fundamentally, he and Lowell were occupied with the same task—that of raising the literary standards of America. In this work, Lowell was the evangelist, preaching to the cultural heathen of America the gospel according to Chaucer and Spenser. Poe was rather the prophet, denouncing literary vices and pointing the moral of his sermons by dealing out resounding thwacks on the heads of literary sinners. His text, stated by himself, was plain enough.

As a literary people, we are one vast perambulating humbug. . . . We should have no trouble in pointing out today some twenty or thirty so-called literary personages, who, if not idiots, as we half think them, or if not hardened to all shame by a long course of disingenuousness, will now blush, in the perusal of these words, through consciousness of the shadowy nature of the purchased pedestal upon which they stand. With the help of a hearty good will, even *we* may yet tumble them down.[4]

Against humbuggery, quackery, puffing, against bad books and bad authors, Poe waged unceasing and bitter war. No one can accuse him of any slowness in bidding quacks go to the devil. Here are some of the critical bricks he hurled.

The simple truth is, Mr. Downing never committed a greater mistake in his life than when he fancied himself a poet, even in the ninety-ninth degree. (That for the author of *Powhatan, an Epic.*)

There are twenty young men of our acquaintance who make no pretence to literary ability, yet who would produce a better book in a week. (And that for the still-remembered Captain Marryat.)

As history this work is invaluable; as a novel, it is well-nigh worthless. (Oh, heresy! He speaks of James Fenimore Cooper, the American Scott.)

Without design, without shape, without beginning,

[4] This was a definite and wholesome reaction from the tendency of the *North American* school of critics, which we have previously noted, to praise all American authors without much discrimination.

middle, or end, what earthly object has this book accomplished? (*Hyperion,* by Henry Wadsworth Longfellow.)

What is *The Vision of Rubeta* more than a vast gilded swill-trough, overflowing with *Dunciad* and water?

We can readily forgive a man for being a fool if he only be a perfect fool—and this is a particular in which we cannot put our hands upon our hearts and say that Mr. Headley is deficient.

Drake's *American Flag,* which still survives in school readers, "owes its high and undeserved reputation to our patriotism—and not to our judgment." Most charming, perhaps, of all, are Poe's verdicts on that gloomy bore, William Harrison Ainsworth. *The Tower of London* is "a somewhat ingenious mixture of pedantry, bombast, and rigmarole. . . . The writer keeps us in a perpetual state of preparation for something magnificent, but the something magnificent never arrives. . . . If ever, indeed, a novel were less than nothing, that novel is *Guy Fawkes.*" (I like that; I once read *Guy Fawkes.*)

One might go on indefinitely with such quotations. For nearly eleven years this warfare against literary idiocy was the main business of Poe's life. The Brook Farm colony, the novels of G. P. R. James, the Boston literary clique, even such consecrated objects as *Pilgrim's Progress* and *Paradise Lost* received attention from his critical flail. All this seems to us now like an unnecessary belaboring of dead horses. But in its day it was a most salutary work. One of the critical vices of the period was its excessive receptivity. The prevailing notion of the day seems to have been that any American who could write verse that would scan was a poet. To the havoc worked by this notion Lowell's essay on Percival gives eloquent and humorous testimony; against that notion, Poe resolutely set his face, with very definite results.

V

But important and valuable though this process of demolishing shaky reputations was, it is not the best nor the most important side of Poe's criticism. His particular excellence as a critic lies in his almost unique ability to apply a keen and marvellously logical thinking machine to the problems of literary theory. When there is a question of pronouncing on the merits of a particular author, intelligence is not enough. There Poe often fails. But criticism does not consist merely of bringing authors before a court of review and there passing judgment on their evil deeds. It also has its philosophical and scientific side. And here Poe excels. Looking over as much of the field of literature as he knew, he constantly exercised his powers of analysis to induce from literary phenomena the general laws that govern them. Up to that time, nothing like this had been attempted in American literary criticism. The earliest American critics, as we have noted, merely parroted Eighteenth Century theories. Dana and Lowell echoed Coleridge and Shelley. Poe was the first American critic to study literature scientifically, to attempt to see for himself the laws behind the phenomena.

In this, as in his reviews of contemporaries, Poe was injured by his lack of scholarship. The task of the literary generalizer is analogous to that of the natural scientist. Gathering as many facts as he can amass, he must endeavor to discover in them some common denominator, some guiding principle. Obviously, the value of his generalization will depend largely on the completeness of his collection of facts. Poe's collection was woefully incomplete. In the English and American literature of his own day he was well read, but of English literature previous to the Nineteenth Century he knew very little. He had read Shakespeare, of course, and some of the Elizabethan dramatists, Milton, and a few Eighteenth Century writers. With French literature he seems to have made himself fairly familiar. Latin he had studied at school. But this is very limited reading for a practicing critic, and even this reading was done in an unsystematic way that deprived it of much of its possible value. Nowhere does Poe give much evidence of possessing the historic sense—that invaluable corrective of hasty opinions. That with such an imperfect equipment as this, Poe managed to develop theories so essentially sound, is one of the greatest evidences of the innate power of his mind.

His theory of criticism can best be set forth by standing aside and allowing Poe to speak for himself.

Of one who instructs we demand, in the first instance, a certain knowledge of the principles which regulate the instruction.

When we attend less to authority and more to principles, when we look less at merit and more at demerit, we shall be better critics than we are.

Criticism is not an essay, nor a sermon, nor an oration, nor a chapter in history, nor a philosophical speculation, nor a prose-poem, nor an art-novel, nor a dialogue. We would wish to limit literary criticism to comment on Art. A book is written, and it is only as the book that we subject it to review. With the opinions of the author the critic really has nothing to do. It is his part simply to decide upon the mode in which these opinions are brought to bear. And this art now no more than in the days of the *Dunciad* can, without neglect of its duty, dismiss errors of grammar, or hand over an imperfect rhyme or a false quantity to the proof-reader.

In general, we should not be overscrupulous about niceties of phrase, when the matter in hand is a dunce to be gibbeted. Speak out—or the person may not understand you. He is to be hung? Then hang him by all means; but make no bow where you mean no obeisance, and eschew the droll delicacy of the Clown in the play—"Be so good, sir, as to rise and be put to death."

There is something like a whole system of criticism contained in these brief passages; not a rounded and complete system, but a system, none the less. Furthermore, Poe, unlike the vast majority of critics, actually made his system work.

Underlying all his theories of literature there is an implicit division of literature into two classes—one appealing mainly to the intelligence, the other directed purely at the emotions.[5] In the first class we find the novel and the drama, in the second the short story and the lyric. The longer forms of poetry, it will be noted, have place in neither class; Poe does not recognize the long poem as a literary form. For each of the four forms here classified, Poe has a theory.

Although a good half of his reviews deal with

[5] This is, of course, merely a restatement of De Quincey's famous classifications of the Literature of Knowledge and the Literature of Power.

novels, his theory of the novel is the least complete of the four. But one can readily reconstruct the outlines of it from scattered observations. Of plot, Poe has a very high notion, as his definition shows; it is "that in which no part can be displaced without ruin to the whole." This approaches somewhat Lowell's doctrine of organic unity in the poem. Plot is to Poe not merely a vehicle for carrying along a number of characters, but an end in itself. He is interested in it as an manifestation of the author's skill; the pleasure he gets from it is the purely intellectual delight of contemplating good workmanship. But he realizes, nevertheless, that plot is not essential to the novel. However, the novel that lacks such a complex and carefully constructed framework must be "a work of genuine realism." Thus early, Poe had arrived at the now accepted division of novels into novels of plot and novels of character.[6] Unfortunately, he did not define what he meant by realism. I should like to hazard a guess that he vaguely anticipated the modern distinction between realism and naturalism. Such a statement as the following, taken in conjunction with his

[6] This distinction between romance and realism in the novel is not, as we sometimes think, a modern invention. One finds the whole matter present, directly or by implication in Simm's preface to *The Yemassee,* published in 1835. Poe may have found the notion there.

frequent remarks about truth and nature in the novel, seems to point that way.

> In my view, if an artist must paint decayed cheeses, his merit will lie in their looking as little like decayed cheeses as possible.

However that may be, Poe invariably finds fault with novelists under two heads—inconsistency of plot or unnaturalness of characterization.

Akin to his theory of the novel is his theory of the drama. That he has such a thing is in itself surprising. No one, as far as I am aware, has ever mentioned Poe as a critic of the drama. Quantitatively, he had very little to do with the drama; there are only eight dramatic reviews, totaling some fifty pages, in the six volumes of his collected works. But because Poe was the kind of critic who cannot examine anything without seeking to explain it, these bits of articles contain the elements of a theory of the theatre. They are easily seventy-five years in advance of their time.

Alone in his day, Poe realized that the drama is, of all literary forms, the one that calls loudest for realistic treatment. He continually demanded greater reality on the stage, continually attacked theatricality in all its forms—the hackneyed plot, the standard tricks of melodrama, the artificial expository device, the set type of character—all of which belonged to the stock in trade of the professional dramatist of his day. Although a lover of plot for plot's sake, or rather, of plot for construction's sake, he roundly declared that the complicated intrigue is a dramatic error.

> It is not an essential. In its intense artificiality it may even be conceived injurious in a certain degree (unless constructed with consummate skill) to that real *life-likeness* which is the soul of the drama of character.

Thus in a sentence he anticipates the thought of 1890.

Still more remarkable, he had the courage to apply the test of reality to the classics of the theatre. It is a well-known fact in literary history that during the first half of the Nineteenth Century the drama in England and America was stunted, almost killed, by that exaggerated worship of the Elizabethans introduced by Charles Lamb, and carried to its reductio ad absurdum by Swinburne. In 1844, Lowell brought this doctrine of Elizabethan perfection to America in his excessively laudatory chapters on Ford and Chapman in *Conversations on Some of the Old Poets*. But in 1845, when this religion was at its undisputed height, Poe remarked, casually, in the course of a two page notice of Hazlitt:

> The drama has not declined as many suppose. It has only been left out of sight by everything else. We must discard all models. The Elizabethan theatre must be abandoned. We need thought of our own—principles of dramatic action drawn not from the old dramatists but from the fountain of a nature that can never grow old.

Thus by seventy-five years he anticipated William Archer. Not only did he attack in this fashion the demi-gods of early romanticism; he even strolled into the temple and disrespectfully thumbed his nose at the deity himself; he dared to question the celestial perfection of Shakespeare.

> "We talk of Hamlet the man," he said, "instead of Hamlet the *dramatis persona*—of Hamlet that God, in place of Hamlet that Shakespeare created. It is not then the inconsistencies of the acting man which we have as a subject of discussion (although we proceed as if it were, and thus inevitably err) but the whims and vacillations, the conflicting energies and indolences of the poet."

That sort of common sense is uncommon enough now; it was shocking heresy in 1845.

In one other respect Poe shows himself, as a dramatic critic, far ahead of his time. Paying no attention to the horrible distinction, common in his day and throughout the greater part of his century, between the literary drama, written only to be read, and the acted drama, a thing not to be considered seriously by true critics, he treated all drama that came his way as something devised for actual performance on the stage. On one occasion, he received for review a copy of a forgotten play by a forgotten authoress—Mrs. Mowatt's *Fashion*.[7] He read it and wrote the review. On the next night he went to see the play performed, found that many of his impressions received from reading were wrong, and wrote a second review, correcting his first judgments in the light of the stage performance. Carrying the same principle to its logical conclusion, he condemned on the one hand revivals of the Greek tragedy, as something no longer suited to the modern stage, and declared, on the other, that the so-called closet drama, the pet of Byron, Tennyson, and Browning, was a bastard form.

Poe has been called the inventor of the short story. The ascription is highly doubtful. Certainly, however, he was the first critic to discuss the short story as an independent literary form. His half-dozen pages of theorizing on the subject are as important

[7] This play was revived in 1929.

to the theory of the short story as Aristotle's *Poetics* to the theory of the drama. Every work that has been written on the same subject since his time has either amplified or contradicted his notion. This notion is, in brief, that the short story should be constructed with the single aim of producing one single effect, evoking one single mood. Its particular characteristic, its distinguishing virtue, is in its unity, its air of totality. Everything in the story should contribute to that effect. The result should be, what he considers the novel because of its length cannot be, a perfect and complete work of art. On this tiny foundation of theory has been built the enormous structure of the modern short story.[8]

VI

Now all the literary doctrines we have so far noted have one characteristic in common. They are all purely incidental or casual in their occurrence. That, I think, is the main reason why they have been so generally overlooked. They are buried away

[8] I know of no better exercise in criticism than to read, side by side Longfellow's review of *Twice Told Tales* and the review of the same volume by Poe, in which the above theories are contained. The one is by a man who is trying to say something pleasant about a friend; the other by a critic who knows his business.

in the most inaccessible places; one plods through page after page of plot summary and grammatical fault-finding to come suddenly upon one brief, flashing sentence that kills, once and for all, some senile literary fallacy, or states, with as near finality as is possible in such matters, a lasting law of literature. It is otherwise with Poe's most important body of literary theory—his principles of poetry. These are gathered into two well-known essays, *The Poetic Principles* and *The Philosophy of Composition.* Over these essays, critical wars innumerable have raged. Regardless of whether we agree with his principles or not, they are at least worth careful examination.

Poe begins by attempting the impossible. He tries to define poetry. But being a wiser man than some critics give him credit for being, he fashions not one definition, but several. Poetry is the product of "the Faculty of Ideality." The poetic sentiment is "the sense of the beautiful, of the sublime, and of the mystical." And again, "Poesy is the sentiment of Intellectual Happiness, and the Hope of a higher Intellectual Happiness hereafter." It is "the thirst for supernal beauty." All these definitions shed light on the matter, though none of them is, or is intended to be final. Eventually, Poe sums up the whole matter in a paragraph capable of being expanded into a volume.

> We would define in brief the Poetry of words as the *Rhythmical Creation of Beauty*. Beyond the limits of Beauty its province does not extend. Its sole arbiter is Taste. With the intellect or with the Conscience it has only collateral relations. It has no dependence, unless incidentally, upon either Duty or Truth.

Here, most critics of Poe seem to have stopped reading, and jumped at once at the conclusion that he was calling for a poetry completely detached from all moral or intellectual qualities. He has merely said, with perhaps greater emphasis, what every sound critic of poetry has said, that poetry is neither a sermon nor a philosophical treatise. Poe goes on to explain that truth and passion may both be part of the subject matter of a poem, but that they must be strictly subordinated to beauty, thus approaching very near to Wordsworth's "emotion recollected in tranquillity."

After laying this foundation, Poe becomes more specific. The Faculty of Ideality is not in itself enough. The merit of the poem lies in conveying the impression of that faculty to the reader. The test of poetic success is in its art—its careful, conscious art. Then, approaching the matter from the psychological side, from the effect on the reader, Poe concludes that a poem, to attain its maximum effect, to have the unity of a perfect work of art, must be capable of being read through at a sitting.[9] A so-called long poem, therefore, is merely a succession of short poems, bound together with links of prose. Furthermore, and here one sees a bit into Poe's own mind, the most poetic tone is a gentle melancholy.

Obviously, this is not the whole story. A definition of poetry that rules out Pope and Chaucer and Shakespeare and most of Burns is not quite satisfactory. Nevertheless, there is a great deal of truth in it, even in the remarks about the long poem. And if for poetry we substitute *lyric* poetry, we will be pretty close to absolute truth.

With his customary logicality, Poe complemented these essays with *The Rationale of Verse*, which deals purely with the mechanics of poetry. And there, except for his curious aberration in regard to the scansion of Latin verse, he is, I think, wholly sound and almost wholly original.

The tantalizing thing about all this is, of course, that it is only a sample of what Poe might have done. The man really had something to say. Given leisure,

[9] Poe got this from Coleridge's *Biographia Literaria.*

given twenty years in which to study and remedy his ignorance, given even a decent home and freedom from wondering where the next meal was coming from, there are no limits to what he might have accomplished.

VII

Even as he was, he remains a great critic. He raised bumps on the heads of more literary idiots than any other man of his time. He formulated, earlier than any other American critic, a consistent and comprehensible theory of criticism. He laid down principles of the drama three quarters of a century ahead of his time. He made the short story a respectable form of literature. Finally, he worked out a theory of poetry that, with certain modifications, is the soundest that this country has produced, topping it with a prosody that leaves most of the syllable counting systems simply nowhere. For most of us, that would be a fair life's work.

Just as Poe and Lowell form in their lives and works an almost perfect antithesis, so do they in their positions in the history of American literary criticism, Lowell, beginning to write in the literary center of America, carrying on in his early work the traditions of Longfellow and Dana, publishing in the great organ of American literary criticism, was thus in the main current of American literary ideas. And after his death, his influence continued to be the most potent in forming literary tradition for a considerable time. Poe, on the contrary, stood in definite opposition to the main literary forces of his day. He had no American literary ancestors, he had no immediate literary descendants. But his thought was too powerful to be ultimately obscured, and so throughout the years since his death we find his influence suddenly appearing in the most unexpected places. In two respects, in his severance of art and morality, and in his insistence on the criticism of form, he stood furthest from the general literary thought of his day and country. Both of these ideas reappear in Lowell, though not expressed with quite the same revolutionary emphasis. But they appear again, coupled with the whole of Poe's theory of poetry after thirty years of desuetude, in the pages of Stedman. About the same time, Poe's doctrines of the short story were resurrected by Brander Matthews, and from that time have been continuously quoted. And last of all, in the Twentieth Century, Poe's methods of attack find their imitator in the equally destructive fusillades of H. L. Mencken. Mr. Mencken's discussion of Irvin Cobb, in his first series of *Prejudices,* is perfect Poe in method and in manner.

SELECTED LIST OF THE CRITICAL WRITINGS OF EDGAR ALLAN POE

William Cullen Bryant's Poems	Southern Literary Messenger, January, 1835
Kennedy's *Horse-Shoe Robinson*	Southern Lit. Mess., May, 1835
R. M. Bird's *The Infidel*	Southern Lit. Mess., June, 1835
Fay's *Norman Leslie*	Southern Lit. Mess., December, 1835
Bulwer's *Rienzi*	Southern Lit. Mess., February, 1836
Georgia Scenes, etc.	Southern Lit. Mess., March, 1836
Poems of Joseph Rodman Drake and Fitz-Green Halleck	Southern Lit. Mess., April, 1836
Letter to B——	Southern Lit. Mess., July, 1836
G. P. R. James, *Life of Richelieu*	Southern Lit. Mess., October, 1836
The Posthumous Papers of the Pickwick Club	Southern Lit. Mess., November, 1836
Willis's *Tortesa*	Burton's Gentleman's Magazine, August, 1839
Undine	Burton's Gent. Mag., September, 1839

Longfellow's *Hyperion*	Burton's Gent. Mag., October, 1839
Moore's *Alciphron*	Burton's Gent. Mag., January, 1840
A Notice of W. C. Bryant	Burton's Gent. Mag., May, 1840
Cooper's *Mercedes of Castille*	Graham's Magazine, January, 1841
Macaulay's *Critical and Miscellaneous Essays*	Graham's Magazine, June, 1841
Seba Smith's *Powhatan*	Graham's Magazine, July, 1841
Ainsworth's *Guy Fawkes*	Graham's Magazine, November, 1841
Christopher North's *Critical and Miscellaneous Essays*	Graham's Magazine, January, 1842
Review of New Books	Graham's Magazine, January, 1842
Hawthorne's *Twice Told Tales*	Graham's Magazine, April, 1842; May, 1842
Tennyson's Poems	Graham's Magazine, September, 1842
James Russell Lowell's Poems	Graham's Magazine, March, 1844
Marginalia	Democratic Review, November, 1844; December, 1845
Imitation, Plagiarism	Broadway Journal, March 8, 1845
The New Comedy of Mrs. Mowatt	Broadway Journal, March 28, 1845; April 5, 1845
The *Antigone* at Palma's	Broadway Journal, April 12, 1845

Alfred Tennyson	Broadway Journal, July 19, 1845
The Characters of Shakespeare by William Hazlitt	Broadway Journal, August 16, 1845
The American Drama	American Whig Review, August, 1845
Marginalia	Godey's Ladies' Book, September, 1845
The Philosophy of Composition	Graham's Magazine, April, 1846
The Literati	Godey's Ladies Book, May to October, 1846
Hawthorne's *Twice Told Tales,* etc.	Godey's Ladies' Book, November, 1847
Marginalia	Graham's Magazine, January, 1848; February, 1848
Lowell's *A Fable for Critics*	South. Lit. Mess., February, 1848
The Rationale of Verse	South. Lit. Mess., October, 1848; November, 1848
About Critics and Criticism	Graham's Magazine, January, 1850
E. P. Whipple and other Critics	Graham's Magazine, January, 1850
The Poetic Principle	Sartain's Union Magazine, October, 1850

These articles may be found in the Stedman and Woodberry edition, Chicago, 1895, 10 volumes, or better, in the Virginia edition, New York, 1902, 17 volumes.

CHAPTER IV

Emerson and Margaret Fuller

I

Whether or not to include Emerson at all in a survey of American critics is a rather doubtful question. Critic in a strict sense he was not. To live among books as Poe and Lowell lived, to spend one's life in writing judgments of authors, as they did, would have seemed to Emerson a piece of utter futility. But although his use of books was very different from Lowell's, the man was so permeated with literature, and so much a thinker, that he could hardly escape having some sort of philosophy of literature. Of all his essays, only two, *Shakespeare, or the Poet* and *In Praise of Books,* can strictly be called literary criticism, but nearly everything he wrote abounds in quotations from literature, in literary references, in literary speculations. Primarily a philosopher, and a philosopher to whom books meant so much, it was essential that he should find some place for literature in his philosophical system. And so we can, without great difficulty, gather from the pages of his essays a theory of literature.

Unlike Poe, and perhaps unlike Lowell, he does not view literature as an end in itself. It is rather a means; its use is "to afford us a platform whence we may command a view of our present life, a purchase by which we may move it." He flatly declares that art for art's sake degrades the seeker. The purpose of literature is therefore moral; "all high beauty has a moral element in it." Goethe has not the highest genius because "he is incapable of self-surrender to the moral sentiment."

Combining this doctrine with his other doctrine of the Over-soul, Emerson arrives at this view of the nature of the poet's office. "The universal nature, too strong for the petty nature of the bard, sits on his neck and writes through his hand." The poet, then, in this view, is an irresponsible agent of divine forces. He does not *will* to write a great poem, since "our moral nature is vitiated by any interference of our will." Carrying out this notion, Emerson distinguishes between genius and talent. Genius is religious; the great poets are content with truth.

Like a good Platonist, Emerson is convinced that "poetry was all written before time was." From this follows naturally his doctrine of organic form; form is not something put on the idea, like a dress; form has "instant dependence on soul." All great poems, as written, then, are but manifestations, more or less imperfect, of the great poetic idea; in a passing spirit of impatience with these manifestations, he in one place brushes aside Milton as too literary, and Homer as too literal and historical.[1] Since, then, the poet is but the voice of the world-soul, it necessarily follows that the great poet is "a heart at unison with his time and country." All this, if we must label things, could be called, I suppose, classicism. There was indeed a strong vein of classicism in Emerson's nature. It creeps out in such chance remarks as this— "The line of beauty is the result of perfect economy." It shows up in his insistence that only a few great books are really necessary; that better than reading new books is re-reading old ones. It is revealed in his genuine love for the Greeks, whom, however, he seems to have read only in translation. But that is only one side of Emerson's literary thought.

Living when he did, he could not very well help coming under the influence of the Romantic move-

[1] This is a typical Emersonian outburst. He is generally full of praise for Milton.

ment. There are romantic elements in Emerson's literary taste. It is as a romantic that he values German literature so much more highly than French; a vein of dislike for French thought and French writing crops out at intervals all through his work. Romantic also is his liking for the Elizabethans. He has words of praise for those giants of early romanticism, Wordsworth and Coleridge, though, significantly enough, it is Coleridge the philosopher, rather than Coleridge the poet, whom he values. And in the true high romantic vein is his remark that "Pope and Johnson and Addison write as if they had never seen the face of the country, but had only read of trees and rivers in books." But in spite of these points, Emerson was too thoroughly at odds with the main aims and ends of the romantic writers to make a really good romanticist. I doubt if he learned from them more than one or two things—his love of nature and solitude, and his appreciation of writers of widely differing periods and nationalities.

Toward that other vexed literary question of that day and this, realism, Emerson's attitude is confused and shifting. In one place he appears as the advocate of a thoroughgoing realism. "What we call obscure condition or vulgar society, is that condition and society whose poetry is not yet written." Utterances like this are at the other extreme from the classic emphasis on the necessity of the high and poetic subject. He exalts the romantic writers as against the men of the Eighteenth Century for their superior realism. In a paragraph of *The American Scholar* he thus interprets the work of the romantics, and contrives at the same time to put forth the most eloquent plea for fidelity to nature that we shall find in American criticism before the time of Howells.

The same movement which effected the elevation of what was called the lowest class in the state, assumed in literature a very marked and as benign an aspect. Instead of the sublime and beautiful; the near, the low, the common, was explored and poetized. That, which had been negligently trodden under foot by those who were harnessing and provisioning themselves for long journeys into far countries, is suddenly found to be richer than all foreign parts. The literature of the poor, the feelings of the child, the philosophy of the street, the meaning of household life, are the topics of the time. It is a great stride. It is a sign—is it not? of new vigor, when the extremities are made active, when currents of warm life run into the hands and the feet. I ask not for the great, the remote, the romantic; what is doing in Italy or Arabia; what is Greek art, or Provençal minstrelsy: I embrace the common, I explore and sit at the feet of the familiar, the low. Give me insight into today, and you may have the antique and future worlds.

But he does not hold steadily to this thoroughly realistic position. In quite another spirit he admonished us, "Do not read what you should learn without asking, in the street and the train." One of his most profound likings was for the heroic note in literature, and the heroic and the realistic are apt to be at war—as indeed he perceived, "Go with mean people," he cries, "and you think life is mean. Then read Plutarch, and the world is a proud place." It was this uncertain attitude toward realism, and not any weak minded surrender to the opinions of others, which was responsible for Emerson's initial acceptance, and later rejection of Whitman.

One more literary note we find in Emerson's critical work, a note sonorous and stirring as a trumpet blast. For all his classic elements, for all his admiration of the few great writers, Emerson was too much of an individualist to belong to any school or bow to any authority. And so at times he turns pure iconoclastic impressionist.

One of the last secrets we learn as scholars is to confide in our own impressions of a book. If Aeschylus is that man he is taken for, he has not yet done his office when he has educated the learned of Europe for a thousand years. He is now to approve himself a master of delight to me.

This, of course, closely parallels Lowell's demand for "freshness of sensation," but whereas Lowell immediately hedges, contending that we must have standards, Emerson characteristically states the idea in its extreme form, and leaves it unqualified, forgetful or regardless of the fact that it contradicts an equally extreme statement on the other side, which he has put forth at some other time.

II

However, all these contradictions and inconsistencies do not disqualify Emerson for the office of literary critic. They rather fit him the better for it. Literature, unlike theology, is not organized in a complete and coherent system. It contains many different and almost conflicting kinds of goodness, and a certain amount of haziness and contradiction in critical theory is apt to indicate that the critic will be receptive to a wide variety of authors. This is true of Emerson. His range of liking is extraordinarily wide. But there are certain authors who, because they are continually cropping up in his pages,

I take to be his prime favorites. For Shakespeare he had apparently a genuine passion. There were none of the customary Puritanic reserves in his surrender to Shakespeare; he likes the whole man. Montaigne, Beaumont and Fletcher, Goethe, Plutarch, and—Swedenborg; a diversified company, but these are the writers he quotes.

But when he comes to deal with contemporary writers, it is Emerson's classicism, his impatience with anything short of the best, that is usually uppermost. To Tennyson he gave a great deal of rather unfavorable attention. While the English-speaking world was going into raptures over *In Memoriam*, Emerson coolly remarked that it was "the commonplaces of condolence among good Unitarians in the first week of mourning. The consummate skill of the versification is the sole merit." His conclusion was that Tennyson was "a beautiful half of a poet." The trouble with Dickens is that "his eye rests on surfaces. He has no insight into character." Shelley is "a little unaffecting." "Macaulay's History is full of low merits. So far can Birmingham go." Carlyle "squanders his genius. There is some inequality between his power of painting, which is matchless, and his power of explaining, which satisfies not."

Still lower was his estimate of American literature. With a critical insight unequalled by any man of his time, he announced that all American literature was "derivative." Anticipating in a sentence the iconoclastic critics of the Twentieth Century, he declared that "the mark of American merit is grace without grandeur." That this judgment was the product of no transitory mood is evidenced by the frequency with which we meet it in Emerson. Equally severe were his comments on specific American writers. From puffery and back-scratching he was entirely free, even when he came to speak of personal friends.[2] Bryant, Poe, Irving, even his New England neighbors, Longfellow and Lowell, he relegates to the limbo of the second-rate. One can easily see the reasons, from Emerson's viewpoint, for these condemnations. Less easy to account for is his absolute disregard for Hawthorne.

> Nathaniel Hawthorne's reputation as a writer is a very pleasing fact, because his writing is not good for anything, and this is a tribute to the man.

In one only of his contemporaries and compatriots

[2] This is in sharp contrast with the general tenderness of the New England critics. But this may in part be due to the fact that the judgments on these writers were not meant for publication, but came from the *Journals*.

did Emerson recognize anything like true literary genius, and that one Thoreau.

III

That Emerson had many of the qualities of the great critic is evident. Enthusiasm for literature, wide reading, catholicity of taste, a high standard and a sharp discrimination, independence,—these are all critical qualities of the first order. That he never became a great critic—or indeed, a critic in any sense, was the result of a lack, not of ability, but of desire. He thought other things more important; and he was right. There have been plenty of men equally well qualified to be literary critics; but there is only one Emerson.

However, if we cannot call Emerson a great critic, we must at the very least recognize him as a great critical force. Lowell and the *North American* school constitute the critical orthodoxy of the Nineteenth Century in America. Poe leads one wing of the opposition, what we might call the artistic wing. Emerson is the leader of a second group of heretics, who agree not so much in specific doctrines as in general attitudes, in fundamental philosophy. In his desire to be independent of traditional judgments, in his occasional moods of almost arrogant disregard for the past, in his call for a literature smacking of the soil, in his dislike of the merely pretty, in his impatience with American literature, Emerson is the teacher of Whitman,[3] of Burroughs, and in part, I think, of the realistic novelists and critics of the eighteen-nineties. And as I read the works of John Macy, Carl Van Doren, Van Wyck Brooks, all of the men of the modern iconoclastic school of critics, or even such far-removed persons as V. F. Calverton, I see everywhere traces of the germinating spirit of Emerson.

IV

Unlike Lowell, whose conservatism that grew with age led him to divorce himself from all schools and movements, unlike Poe, whose touchiness of temper and vitriolic pen brought him by the end of his life into an almost savage isolation, Emerson became the teacher of a fairly definite school of critics. One of these demands separate notice; that one is Margaret Fuller.

Margaret Fuller is mentioned in all histories of American Literature, yet as a writer she is as dead as Nahum Tate. Widely accepted in her own day,

[3] No one, I think, can read *Self-Reliance* without being reminded of Whitman at every other sentence. It is almost prophecy. See also a paragraph in essay on "The Poet."

the first woman in this country, I believe, to attempt and succeed in making a living by her pen, there is not a single page of her writing that is read today, except by the literary antiquarian. She survives wholly as a personality, embalmed in the dislike of Lowell and Hawthorne.

Higginson, it is true, calls her the best literary critic of America. She is not that, she is not even a good literary critic, and for one reason. She could not write. Her style is impossible—dull, inflated, muddy, possessing all the vices and none of the virtues of critical prose. And yet, if one has the patience to wade through it, to discover what she was trying to say, one finds traces of a good critical intelligence.

Like Emerson, she was in revolt against Puritanism. Almost the only quotable sentence I have found in her work is an attack on Puritan narrowness.

> Dear New England, region where the tyranny of public opinion is carried to a perfection of minute scrutiny beyond what it ever was before in any age or place.

Like Emerson, she is to be considered as a liberalizing force in American literary opinion. She was entirely free from the moral smugness of the *North*

American school; indeed, she goes out of her way to defend authors under the New England ban. Her greatest admiration—and here the influence of Emerson is plain—was for Goethe, himself no mean liberal, whom she valued above all modern writers. Byron, Shelley, Moore, all *bêtes noires* of contemporary moralists, she contrived to discuss with commendable detachment, praising and blaming on literary grounds alone. Not that she is a literary immoralist; she is too good an Emersonian for that. But she drops the Judaistic moral cant that was the prevailing vice of so much of American literary criticism in her day, setting up in its place a sort of humanitarianism that often leads her into strange enthusiasms, but that is less deforming and dangerous than the other sort.[4]

In her general view of American literature she follows Emerson rather closely, finding it in the main derivative and second-hand. Thus she is unsparing in her condemnation of Longfellow, of whom she accurately says that "the ethical part of his writing has a hollow, second-hand sound." She speaks sharply of Cooper's faults, though she is sure that he has virtues that will cause him to survive,

[4] This humanitarianism leads her, for example, to place Eugene Sue above Balzac, whom she admired on literary grounds.

dismisses Willis as trivial, and has no use at all for Lowell's poetry, which she characterizes as "a copious stream of pleasant sound." This again, is all to her credit. In one respect, indeed, she betters the instruction of her master. She was far more interested than he in literature in the making, and she had a much keener ear for contemporary merit. Thus, with considerable acumen, she picks out Poe and Hawthorne as the best American writers of the day. In this judgment she rises far superior to Emerson, whose characterization of Poe as the "jingle man" and whose contemptuous dismissal of Hawthorne make bad blots on his record as a critic.

It is, I think, highly significant that Margaret Fuller, and Emerson's other follower in the field of criticism, George Ripley, ended by transferring the scene of their critical labors to New York. There, amid the activities of business and the babel of immigrant races, new currents of literary thought were rising, whose development we shall trace in a later chapter.

CRITICAL WRITINGS OF RALPH WALDO EMERSON

Criticism—comment on books and references to books —runs through practically all of Emerson's work. I have here merely noted the places where it is most consolidated.

Nature	James Munroe & Co. Boston, 1836
The American Scholar	James Munroe & Co. Boston, 1837
Milton	*North American Review*, July, 1838
Literary Ethics	C. C. Little & James Brown, Boston, 1838 .
Essays, First Series	James Munroe & Co. Boston, 1841
Essays, Second Series	James Munroe & Co. Boston, 1844
Representative Men	Phillips & Sampson, Boston, 1849
Society and Solitude	Fields, Osgood & Co. Boston, 1870
The Heart of Emerson's Journals	Houghton Mifflin, Boston, 1926

All of these except the last can be most easily found in any of the numerous collected editions of Emerson's works. I give them in their original form merely to indicate the dates.

CRITICAL WRITINGS OF MARGARET FULLER

Papers on Literature and Art 2 vols., Wiley & Putnam, New York, 1846.

Margaret Fuller as a Literary Critic, Helen Q. McMaster, Univ. of Buffalo Studies, 1928.

CHAPTER V

STEDMAN

I

ROUGHLY speaking, the year 1880 marks the shifting of the literary capital of the United States to New York from Boston. Throughout the century, there had been rivalry between these two centers. New York had slightly the advantage in time; the work of Brockden Brown and of Irving antedated any significant literary activity in Boston. But the establishment of the *North American,* and the appearance of the New England group of writers, Emerson, Lowell, Hawthorne, Holmes, Whittier, all of whom revolved about Boston as a center, gave that city the primacy. It was not, however, an undisputed primacy. Poe and Willis and Grant White, all in some sense rebels against the literary orthodoxy of Boston, attempted to make the commercial metropolis a literary capital, though without great success. Finally, in the seventies, as the old group of New England writers died off and no successors rose to take their places, as New York became increasingly important as a financial center, drawing to itself both publishers and authors, the tide began to turn. In 1880, Lowell was abroad; Henry James was still of minor importance; Howells had not yet struck a critical pitch of his own. And so the editors of the *Century Magazine,*[1] which was rapidly assuming the place of the *Atlantic Monthly* as the leading literary organ of the day, cast about for a new leader of criticism. They found him in the New York Stock Exchange.

At no other period, I think, could Edmund Clarence Stedman have been accepted, as without question for a decade and a half he was accepted, as the leading literary critic of America. His biography hardly looks like that of a literary genius. Born in Connecticut, he left New England after being expelled from Yale, ventured for a few years as a minor poet and newspaper man, and finally settled down, in the sixties, to a career of stocks and bonds. For forty years he struggled on as a rather mediocre financier, constantly casting back longing glances at literature, yet never returning, while sympathizing friends shed oceans of tears over his hard fate,

[1] This magazine changed its name, but not its identity. Begun in 1870 as *Scribner's Monthly,* it became in 1880 *The Century Magazine.*

and the waste of his beautiful talent. This is not the kind of career one expects for a literary dictator.

Nor does his actual critical production seem quite up to the reputation it supported. Compared with the work of most famous critics, Stedman wrote very little. Four volumes—*Victorian Poets, Poets of America, The Nature and Elements of Poetry* and *Genius and Other Essays*—constitute his complete critical works. Swell this out with his two anthologies, Victorian and American, with his labors as co-editor of the *Library of American Literature*, and we still have very little to show for him. Of course, mere volume of production counts for nothing. There are critics of one essay, just as there are poets of one poem. Aristotle himself survives in criticism in a slender volume of a hundred pages. All of Poe that is read nowadays you can slip into your pocket. But with Stedman the deficiency in size is counterbalanced by no extraordinary richness of quality. There are no pages in his three volumes that have the magisterial weight of Arnold, the flashing certainty of Hazlitt, the pregnant theorizing of Poe, or the stylistic bravado of Lowell. Stedman is dull reading. His reputation, then, one is forced to believe, is out of all proportion to his actual merit. Here is a mystery—until one realizes that Stedman is one of those fortunate persons who make a reputation, not because they are great, but because they are representative. He sums up, in himself and in his four volumes, a whole stream of tendencies in American literature. He is to be considered, not as a great critic, but as an interesting and indicative symptom.

It was an age of silent revolution in literature, and Stedman was the mildest, quietest, of revolutionaries. Until 1880, American criticism had been written almost wholly in New England. The exceptions, like Poe, were out of the main current, and, as has been pointed out, practically devoid of influence in their time. This New England criticism, the criticism of the early *North American Review*, was marked by the Puritan suspicion of pleasure and beauty as ends, was colored by the Puritan ethical prepossession. The dictum enunciated by the *North American* in 1827, "The theory which treats of beauty as of something independent of Moral effect, is still without advocates among us," could have been reasserted with almost equal truth in the sixties and early seventies. True, both Lowell and Emerson had moved far from the narrowness of extreme Puritanism, but in both these men criticism was still markedly ethical in its aims and judgments. But with Stedman came a change. His ideal, and that of the poets most closely associated with him, Aldrich and Taylor, was beauty for its own sake, Tennysonian finish of workmanship. This is, of course, a very incomplete ideal; it resulted in a good deal of futile prettiness in writing; but it was in the eighties a revolutionary ideal, and perhaps a necessary step in the development of American letters. The cult of Tennyson, the writing of ballades and roundels, the importation of Dobson, Gosse, and Lang through the columns of the *Century*—these were the signs of the times in literary New York. American literature had done with sermons; now was the time for sonnets.

Curiously enough, the root of this revolt of Stedman's from ethics to æstheticism sprang from his acquaintance with the Greek and Latin classics—those strange and wonderful human documents that, in spite of the layers of pedantry under which they are commonly buried, do somehow manage, now and then, to effect the mental liberation of him who loves them. And unlike Lowell, who rendered lip-service to the classics, while he preferred the mediæval writers, Stedman genuinely loved the classics. His pages are filled with classical echoes. One of the dreams of his life was the making of a verse translation of Theocritus. From Theocritus and the Greeks, Stedman learned, as Arnold had learned, to love beauty, to reverence form and finish. In fact, Stedman was trying, in a far feebler way, to preach to the millionaires and corruptionists of the Gilded Age the same gospel of Hellenism that Arnold was so strenuously dinning in the ears of British Philistines.

II

It was the age of gentlemanliness in criticism. The art had traveled a long way since the days of Jeffrey and the Edinburgh Reviewers. Whatever the faults of that group of critics, one always understood what they were trying to say. When they thought an author bad, they said so, very loud and clear. But they had suffered the misfortune of condemning, in very plain terms, certain authors who in 1880 were among the immortals; and thereby they had become infamous. And so the memory of "This will never do" and of the essay that did not kill Keats haunted the critics of the later Nineteenth Century, and they grew afraid to condemn any book, however bad they privately thought it. After all, it might prove to be a great but unperceived work of genius. Thus criticism grew gentler and gentler from year to year. Lowell occasionally revolted, and vented some of his temper on a Percival; but Stedman's soft-spokenness never failed. This was not a matter of temperament only. Stedman was gentle on principle. Of Poe's criticism, which was not notable for its sweetness, he remarked: "I hold it a sign of progress that criticism by force of arms would now be less effective."

It is curious to observe the workings of this gentle theory of criticism when applied to Longfellow. Reading carefully between the lines, one eventually makes out the fact that Stedman recognized Longfellow as a second-rate poet.[2] But there is not a sentence in Stedman's essay on Longfellow which could give pain to Longfellow's most devoted admirer. The chapter opens in a peculiarly apologetic strain, deprecating the attacks which had been made on the poet.[3] Stedman goes on to explain Longfellow's alleged plagiarisms as a necessary step in the importation of European culture. And his didacticism is likewise excused as a necessary sugar-coating, for an American audience, of the unsavory

[2] It is frequently assumed that Longfellow was generally accepted, until recently, as the great American poet of his day. As a matter of fact, no American critic of size ever gave Longfellow anything but very qualified praise.

[3] In his letters, Stedman remarks, "The hard fact is that everyone of his [Longfellow's] poems and lyrics reflects somebody else's poem or lyric."

pill of undiluted beauty. Of *Evangeline,* Stedman remarks:

> There are flaws and petty fancies and homely passages in *Evangeline;* but this one poem, thus far the flower of American idylls, known in all lands, I will not approach in a critical spirit. There are rooms in every house where one treads with softened footfall.

A very pretty sentiment, but when criticism thus abdicates its functions, it becomes nothing at all. Yet here and there Stedman lets his real opinions peep out. There is a hint of sharpness in the little aside, "He [Longfellow] often taught by choice the primary class." It seems perfectly clear to me, after several readings of the essay, that Stedman knew exactly what was the matter with Longfellow—that he saw plainly Longfellow's lack of vitality and profound passion, his platitudinousness of thought, his excessive bookishness, his weak didacticism. But the knowledge was well-concealed, and one can praise Stedman's taste only at the expense of his critical sincerity.[4]

Whittier received similar treatment. Stripped of its verbiage, the chapter dealing with him really

[4] This opinion is borne out by a reading of Stedman's letters, where he damns bad authors with an explicitness altogether foreign to his published work.

says that he wasn't much of a poet, but that the critic, considering his exemplary life and devotion to a great cause, should overlook mere poetic failings. And again, criticism abdicates.

Stripped of its verbiage—that implies a great deal, for Stedman is of all critics the most verbose. His thought is concealed under page after diffuse page of prettily turned, impressive sounding, but almost meaningless sentences. There are two reasons for this diffuseness, verbosity, muddiness. The first is the continual conflict going on in Stedman's mind between his critical taste, which was both sound and sure, and his principle of speaking softly. Stylistically, he is the exact opposite of Matthew Arnold. Reading Arnold, one often feels that the writer is in positive agony lest his meaning should not be perfectly clear. Stedman seems to fear equally that his opinions might become known. He is continually forced by his principles and attitude into apologizing, palliating, excusing, toning down.

The second cause of this stylistic muddiness is that strange critical tradition, which still prevails, that when one criticizes poetry one must do it in poetic prose. This tradition originated, I believe, with Shelley; it nearly wrecked Lowell in his earlier days; it quite ruined Swinburne as a critic. With Stedman it became a positive vice. Like the elegant periphrasts of the Eighteenth Century, he never calls a spade a spade. A poet is a "bard," or a "singer," or even a "minnesinger." A group of poets is a "choir." Particularly poetic, in their richness of imagery, their splendor of diction, are the sentences with which Stedman opens his essays.

It is my design to trace the current of poesy, deepening and widening in common with our streams of riches, knowledge, and power; to show an influence upon the national sentiment no less potent, if less obvious than that derived from the historic records of the past; to watch the first dawning upon an eager people of the happy, heavenly vision men call Art; to observe closely and to set down with an honest hand our foremost illustrations of the Rise of Poetry in America. Such is my purpose, and I deem it not a mean one.

Listening to the concert of modern song, a critical ear detects the note of one voice which possesses a distinct quality and is always at its owner's command.

Death has summoned with his impartial touch young and old alike from the cycle of poets considered in our original review. [With the touching marginal comment, "Stilled Voices."]

III

The earliest, the best known, and the most valuable of Stedman's critical volumes is *Victorian*

Poets, published in 1875. In this volume Stedman applies to the study of Victorian poetry something of the method of Taine, attempting to trace general tendencies in the period, and to account for these tendencies by social, economic, and intellectual changes. In part, this is excellently done. Stedman's labelling and characterization of the "idyllic" method, his demonstration that the greater part of Victorian poetry is the result of a crossing of Wordsworth and Keats, are excellent critical hits. The extended parallel of Tennyson and Theocritus is a genuine piece of comparative criticism. The chapter on Landor, whom Stedman, both by his classical sympathies and by his admiration for pure finish of form, was well-fitted to appreciate, is at once Stedman's masterpiece, and the best critique of Landor that I have seen. But as soon as Stedman leaves the regions of pure appreciation and ventures into discussions of intellectual currents, neither his mind nor his style will stand the strain. His discussions of the effect of scientific agnosticism on Tennyson, of religious doubt on Arnold, of the revolutionary spirit and the neo-pagan movement on Swinburne, are pitifully inadequate. He was the first American critic to be conscious of the effect of science on contemporary thought; that much is to his credit. But to handle a topic like the relation of poetry to science, which bothered Stedman greatly, and to which he devoted a large section of the introductory chapter of this volume, demands precision of thought and clear-cut sharpness of statement. The quality of Stedman's remarks may be deduced from the passage quoted below.

A pagan saw the morning as Guido has painted it. The Sun God in very truth was urging on his fiery-footed steeds. The clouds were his pathway; the early morning Hour was scattering in advance flowers of infinite prismatic hues, and her blooming and radiant sisters were floating in air around Apollo's chariot; the earth was roseate with celestial light; the blue sea laughed beyond. Swiftly ascending Heaven's archway, the retinue swept on; all was real, exuberant life and gladness; the gods were thus waiting upon humanity, and men were the progeny of the gods.

This is neither good sense nor good prose.

There are other blemishes in the book. The chapters on the minor poets are very apt to degenerate into mere catalogues of almost forgotten names. There is always in evidence Stedman's desire to have a kind word for everyone. One finds it hard to forgive his lumping together in one chapter, and treating as of equal value, Hood, Arnold, and Bryan

Waller Procter. But for all that, the book is certainly the most inclusive, and probably the most valuable survey of Victorian poetry that has yet been made.

IV

It was not until ten years later, in 1885, that Stedman found time to leave the bulls and bears at their antics, and to produce his second volume, *Poets of America.* In this volume, in which he passes in review the leaders of American poetry from Bryant to Bayard Taylor, Stedman manifests, even more fully than in his former work, his peculiar critical characteristics. While the tone of *Victorian Poets* is usually gentle, it does occasionally mount into something like a vigorous attack on poetic vices. Mrs. Browning is rather severely handled; her husband is attacked for his barbarism of taste. But these were foreign poets, viewed with the detachment of distance. One can say of them with impunity things one hesitates to say of one's contemporaries and compatriots. And for all his revolt, Stedman was still susceptible to the pressure of the New England tradition. It may have been the contact of the literary world about him; it may have been merely the desire to avoid giving pain to a number of estimable and still-living gentlemen; it may be that soft-spokenness, like other vices, grows with age—whatever the cause, *Poets of America* has less of severity, less of condemnation, more of a positively radiant kindness, than any other volume of criticism published.[5]

The critic, says John Middleton Murry, should not like too many things. His judgment should be selective; it is a part of his business to set up an unattainable ideal, and to refuse to be satisfied with anything short of it. If this be the true notion of the critic, Stedman is a very bad critic indeed. Rare is the poet in whom he cannot find some excellence worth praising. Throughout his work, one can find no trace of a genuinely violent dislike. Thus, his survey of American poetry stands at the opposite extreme from Emerson's. And yet, this comprehensiveness was not altogether a defect; it was a part of Stedman's function, as a literary dictator, to help in the freeing of American letters from the narrowness of preceding generations. And in this work his inclusiveness was something of a help. It

[5] Contrast with the handling of Bryant in this volume, the following sentence from Stedman's letters: "We are going to have a stilted and heavy translation of Homer, by Bryant, out this winter, and all the geese are going to praise it. Bryant is too Latinesque to translate the swift and racy Iliad."

preserved him from Lowell's great weakness—a total failure to recognize genius under new forms. Although Stedman's own preferences were for the productions of the art-school, for work of the Keats-Poe-Tennyson type, he could see the weakness of that form, and the possibilities of good work in other forms. Alone in his day he perceived, and stated repeatedly, although without the emphasis necessary to catch the ear of his contemporaries, that the art-school was dying of inanition, that the idyllic method had been worked to its limit; and in spite of his love for that method, he saw clearly that what poetry most needed was an infusion of new life and passion. He censured, very mildly, of course, the coolness of Tennyson, the passionlessness of Longfellow, the hot-house scents of Poe, the eclecticism of Taylor, and hailed, as the best augury for the future, the work of Whitman.

It is a relief to turn from the critical beating-about-the-bush which forms so large a part of *Poets of America* to the chapter on Whitman. Here Stedman, free from the traditions which he disliked, yet against which he did not venture to revolt openly, exhibited himself at his best. The critic whose major admirations are Theocritus and Landor and Tennyson, and yet who can thoroughly give himself up to Whitman, is not the commonest of phenomena. The essay, indeed, is one of that rarest of things in the history of criticism—the tribute of a lover of a recognized and conventional sort of excellence to an excellence of a new and disturbing kind. And in paying this tribute, Stedman was performing the most daring act of his life. There had been found critics to say a favorable word for Whitman before this. But they were men like Burroughs and Conway, heretics, rebels, outcasts. Stedman was the first critic generally accepted by the American public who took up the cudgels for Walt. One element in Whitman, to be sure, Stedman did not like. Idealist that he was, he could hardly be expected to take great pleasure in Whitman's daring excursions into the realm of the carnal.[6] But that, after all, is a matter of taste, even yet. Aside from that, the essay is filled with critical dicta of surprising insight. I suspect that one reason why Stedman was so willing to accept Whitman came from the fact that he viewed Whitman's form, not as something new and strange, but as a revival of a very old tradition. Indeed, he specifically connects Whitman with the translators of the King James version. He realized,

[6] "Let no man write a line he would not have his daughter read." Stedman's Letters.

as every one realizes now, but as few did in the eighties, that Whitman was not the apostle of formlessness, but the owner of a distinctive form of his own, the demonstrator of a very definite technique. And he cleverly noted that in spite of all Whitman's efforts to be the poet of a democracy, his poetry was not a poetry of the people, but a poetry that appeals mainly to a public so thoroughly acquainted with the traditional forms as to be weary of them, and eager to try some new thing. The concluding paragraph of the essay, with its careful balancing of praise and blame, its definiteness and soundness of idea, is a tiny masterpiece, sufficient of itself to place Stedman, not among the great critics, but among the great might-have-beens of criticism.

V

For seven years after the writing of *Poets of America* Stedman kept silence. Finally, in 1892, his third and last volume appeared.[7] All his life—all, that is, except the part devoted to the stock exchange—Stedman had given to the study of poetry. He had read poetry, read enormously and wisely.

[7] *Ge[illegible]s and Other Essays* was collected from magazines and published after his death.

He had written poetry himself. He had, in his two previous volumes, surveyed minutely the poetry of England and America in the Nineteenth Century. He now planned a final volume, his master-work, which should perform the task so often attempted by critics great and small, from Aristotle down, yet never carried out with any final and complete success. He would construct a theory of poetry—a *Poetics*. The result was the volume bearing the imposing title, *The Nature and Elements of Poetry*. It is a volume that one opens with considerable apprehension. The process of literary abstraction, the formation of a theory of poetry, demands the utmost clarity of thought, the utmost precision of expression. Now Stedman is conspicuous for the lack of just these qualities. He was, apparently, doomed to failure from the start.

The book is diffuse. There are, stretching through it, vast Saharas of words. The whole first chapter is a dull, stupid, and rather pointless delimitation of the provinces of science and poetry—Stedman's old difficulty. And yet, this is, in general, Stedman's best piece of prose writing, often clear-cut, abounding in sharp-edged statements, fairly well-stripped of Stedman's usual would-be poetic figures of speech. This is in large part due to the fact that the book was first delivered as a series of lectures at Johns Hopkins.

But not even the influence of the lecture halls of Johns Hopkins can account for the sudden growth in ideas which this book evidences; for the book has ideas, sensible, logically developed, far beyond anything of which Stedman had previously shown himself capable. When a man of sixty, whose critical writings have up to that time been rather conspicuous for weakness in reasoning power, turns to one of the most difficult tasks in the field of criticism, and develops in the course of that task such unexpected ability to think as is manifested in this volume, we have either a miracle or a mystery. Not that the ideas here set forth are inconsistent with Stedman's earlier criticism in fundamental attitude. The main thesis of the volume, the thesis that was implicit in his earlier critical works, is that poetry is the creation of pure beauty, independent of all considerations of moral effect. He sounds again in this volume, though softly, the tocsin of the anti-Puritan revolt. He asserts, in opposition to Puritan suspicion of the emotions, that passion is an end in poetry, a good in itself. He handles very neatly the question of didacticism, arriving eventually at the conclusion that "a prosaic moral is injurious to virtue by making it repulsive"—about as sensible an utterance on that vexed question as any critic has made, and one that has the added advantage of turning the moralist's guns against himself. All this is, of course, quite consistent with Stedman's earlier work. But the new and strange feature of the volume is the constructive ability with which a theory of poetry is framed to include these ideas.

The key to the mystery is Poe. Stedman had long been a student of Poe. He had collaborated with Professor Woodberry in writing a life of Poe. He was probably one of the few scholars of his day who were acquainted with Poe's critical writings. And in his acquaintance with those writings lies the reason for his sudden growth in ideas. *The Nature and Elements of Poetry* is nothing more nor less than *The Poetic Principle* and *The Rationale of Verse*, enormously expanded in expression, profusely illustrated by quotations from poets ancient and modern, with a few errors removed, and a few sharp edges filed off.

This is a serious charge, but the evidence lies plain before us. The nature of Stedman's handling of Poe is well suggested by the definitions of poetry formulated by the two men. Poe says, "Poetry is the rhythmical creation of beauty." Stedman repeats, expanding, "Poetry is rhythmical, imaginative language, expressing the invention, taste, thought, passion, and insight, of the human soul." Stedman did in some respects alter Poe's principles—not for the better. He added to the elements of poetry, passion, so strangely, and perhaps so wisely ruled out by Poe.[8] He lightly waved aside Poe's statement that there is no such thing as a long poem. But in most respects the correspondence between the two is perfect. In his insistence on concrete beauty as "the one indispensable in poetry"; in his unfailing opposition to didacticism; in the major articles of his poetic creed, Stedman repeated Poe exactly. "Evanescence," says Stedman, "is an unfailing cause of charm. Sorrow and regret are the most effective of poetic emotions. The sweetest sound in music is a dying fall." This is Poe, at his most idiosyncratic point. Straight from Poe comes Stedman's distinction between the Fancy and the Imagination; he even borrowed Poe's illustrations of the contrasted qualities—*The Culprit Fay* and some lines out of Shelley.

There is, of course, no reasonable objection to Stedman's making use of Poe. Indeed, he deserved

[8] I do not think that Stedman fully comprehended Poe's reason for this ruling. See the chapter on Poe for an expansion of Poe's ideas.

something of Poe, for it is in large part due to his services, both as editor and as critic, that Poe's reputation was preserved through a period of general neglect. That Stedman recognized the excellence of Poe's theories of poetry is one of the many bits of evidence that lead one to conclude that his critical taste and judgment, when allowed to function freely, were unusually good. But to borrow thus wholesale, and to make no acknowledgment, is the clearest illustration of that lack of intellectual honesty which deforms all of Stedman's critical work.[9]

VI

That Stedman has many of the qualities of a great critic is unquestionable. His theory of poetry—stolen though it was—is as satisfactory as any such theory is apt to be; his reading, within his limited field of poetry, was immense; his love and enthusiasm unfailing; his taste both sure and catholic. His contribution to the advance of American literature, by his recognition of such unpopular geniuses as Poe and Whitman; by his constant advocacy of a more civilized view of literature; by his opposition to the Puritanic blight on art; by his praise of

[9] He calls his work "a pioneer attempt, in these parts, to set forth the canons of the poetic art"—knowing, all the while, what Poe had done.

beauty and workmanship for their own sake; lastly, by his prophetic forecast of a new school of poets when he saw that the art-school had done its work —his contribution was of genuine value. But for all that, he has left us nothing which entitles him to rank with the great critics—with Hazlitt and Sainte-Beuve and Arnold, or with Lowell and Henry James among his own countrymen. Potentially great in many respects, he failed of attaining greatness in criticism. Part of this failure was due to his conformity to a vicious critical tradition; more to his own defects—mental weakness, lack of courage to speak his mind, intellectual dishonesty. For twenty years he was one of the great names in American criticism. Today there remain of him only the portrait of a strikingly handsome man, a colorless page or two in the *Cambridge History,* two useful but impersonal anthologies, and four blue volumes gathering dust on the library shelves.

But Stedman is to be considered not merely as an individual, nor even as the recorder of a shift in literary geography. He was also the voice of a creative school. The theories enunciated by him in his critical work were precisely the theories being put into practice by the group of poets among whom he lived and worked. Taylor, Stoddard, Boker, Read,

Aldrich, these were the men for whom Stedman spoke. There is a singular contrast between the work of these men and the age and country in which they lived. It was the age of Reconstruction and P. T. Barnum, of the Grant administration and the Standard Oil, of Boss Tweed and Commodore Vanderbilt, of the Ku Klux Klan and the Molly Maguires—the ugliest age that America has seen. Disgusted with the world around them, these men deliberately turned their backs on it, and built them a little walled garden, in which to write such poems as *Friar Jerome's Beautiful Book,* and *Prince Deucalion,* and *Alectryon,* and the *Bedouin Love Song.* Sometimes a process like this produces great poetry. In their case, it produced nothing but futility. Indeed, American poetry was going to sleep. The earlier New England poets had ceased to produce. The art-school, was, as Stedman himself realized and wrote, dying of its own emptiness. In Whitman the voice of a new age was sounding, but he was only a voice crying in a wilderness of neglect. And after Stedman, indeed, during his lifetime, American criticism reflected the change in creative work, and definitely turned from the consideration of American poetry. To the great critics of the earlier day—Poe, Lowell, Emerson,—poetry had been the major interest. With Stedman it was the sole interest. But after Stedman, no American critic of the first rank gave much attention to the criticism of poetry. The novel was coming into its own.

CRITICAL WRITINGS OF EDMUND CLARENCE STEDMAN

Tennyson and Theocritus	Atlantic Monthly, November, 1871
Victorian Poets	Houghton Mifflin, Boston, 1875
Poets of America	Houghton Mifflin, Boston, 1885
The Nature and Elements of Poetry	Houghton Mifflin, Boston, 1892

(First published as a series of essays in the *Century Magazine.*)

Genius and Other Essays	Moffat Yard & Co., N. Y., 1911
Life and Letters of E. C. Stedman	Moffat Yard & Co., N. Y., 1910

CHAPTER VI

Henry James

I

Henry James was the first major American critic to give his main attention to the novel. This is significant as indicating the general shift in literary emphasis from poetry to the novel. He was also the first American novelist of importance to write criticism. When the creative artist turns critic, the result is always interesting. But if the creative artist happens to be a man whose strength lies in words and feelings, rather than in thoughts, we read, with something of a shock of disillusionment, such effusions as the *Preface to the Lyrical Ballads,* or *A Study of Shakespeare.* If, on the other hand, the artist happens to have a mind as well as an ear for words, if he is a Coleridge or a Dryden, criticism is enriched by one of its great masterpieces. Now every page of the long series of novels that oozed forth, year after year, from the sedentary study of Henry James, bore the impress of a mind that was above all things critical—a mind reflective, sensitive to beauty, super-civilized, curious both of humanity and of art.

James is not ordinarily ranked with the great critics; indeed, he is not usually thought of as a critic at all. This, I suspect, is largely because his criticism bulks so small beside the ponderous mass of his novels. It consists of but four volumes,—*Hawthorne, French Poets and Novelists, Partial Portraits,* and *Notes on Novelists*—with a few scattering and unimportant essays in periodicals. In spite of this, however; in spite also of the extremely narrow range of his criticism, he deserves to rank with the greatest of American critics.

It is useless to look in Henry James for many of the qualities which we ordinarily expect in the great critic. He had none of that encyclopedic range and curiosity which delight us in Huneker and Sainte-Beuve. He showed none of that passion for the older masters of literature which illuminates the pages of Arnold and Lowell. He lacked the vivacity and impudence of the modern journalistic critic. And yet he is a great critic—though by all odds the narrowest of great critics, even more restricted than Stedman, who, though he confined himself to poetry, evidenced throughout familiarity with the great poets of all lands and ages. Small in volume, the criticism of Henry James is practically confined to one limited topic. Twice—in the essays on Baudelaire and Musset—he touched poets; except for these, his criticism has but one subject—the European novel from 1840 to 1910. His one unfailing topic might be stated thus: "The modern novel as it now is compared with my notion of what it ought to be." And even within this small area, there are curious untouched fields. For the contemporary American novel, or indeed, for the American novel of any time, he seems to have had little regard. The only American novelist whom he discussed was Hawthorne. On the European side, however, he extended the view of American criticism. The tendency of American criticism, when it looked abroad, had been to see only England. Of non-English-speaking novelists only Balzac and Hugo had received much mention from American critics, though we find occasional references to Dumas, Zola, and Eugene Sue. But with James, the novel on the continent was a major interest, and it was a part of his critical function to introduce to the American public such comparatively unknown figures as Gautier and Flaubert, and Maupassant, and, going farther afield, Turgeniev and Tolstoy. For all that, it is a limited field in which he worked; perhaps his very greatness lies in this limitation, and the intensification that goes with it.

II

Criticism, of course, in spite of all the professors and most of the critics, is as personal an art as poetry or theology, and one of the fascinations of the study of criticism lies in the attempt to spy out the critic's personality. While there are many literary personalities more likable than that of Henry James, there are few more interesting. His life was a perpetual example of the great moral principle that no man can step off his own shadow. Despite his long and painstaking effort to become cosmopolitan, to attain the European viewpoint, there always clung to him a faint perfume of colonial America. Particularly was this noticeable in his dealings with his French contemporaries. They were very interesting people, and very clever writers, no doubt, but there was a something—. He confessed that he could never feel quite at home in Paris, nor quite at ease in the circle about Flaubert. And when he came to write of these men, his moralistic bias, the nemesis of so many American critics, was apparent. Nothing else can account for his statement that *Mademoiselle de Maupin* is Gautier's worst book, and that its gloriously rowdy preface is "a puerile performance." Such condemnations grew on the soil of Massachusetts.

But over the New England maple was laid a veneer of polished rosewood. Despite this moralistic trend, James was too well acquainted with civilized literary opinion to be openly moralistic in his critical doctrines. While his condemnation may be the result of moral prejudice, he was always clever enough to mask it by an intelligent rationalization. Thus, the Gautier preface was not vicious, but puerile. Similarly he handled Baudelaire. "Baudelaire is not evil in his own experience, but rather impelled by an intellectual curiosity about evil. His poetry is cold, therefore." And of George Sand he remarked, "She had no moral taste." In contrast to earlier American critics, who were in the habit of calling down fire from heaven on the heads of naughty continental authors, this half-apostasized son of the Puritans damns them with a sneer.

Indeed, there is no master of the critical sneer who approaches Henry James. Where other critics grew shrill-voiced and raucous, he was always cool and superior, always the gentleman, and always able to find intelligent ground for his antipathies. To no author was he so conspicuously unfair as to his compatriot, Poe. Against Poe he manifested something like a personal grudge. One is somewhat at a loss to account for this strange and exceptional bitterness. Perhaps it was a bit of inherited Massachusetts tradition; Poe was never exactly in favor with the Brahmins. But James was far more unfair to Poe than was Lowell, who grew up amid the smoke and heat of the Poe-Longfellow war. Whatever the cause, the antipathy existed. But it is much easier to disagree with James's remarks on Poe than to refute them.

> With all due respect to the very original genius of the author of the *Tales of Mystery,* it seems to us that to take him with more than a certain degree of seriousness is to lack seriousness one's self. An enthusiasm for Poe is the mark of a decidedly primitive stage of reflection.

Now the diabolical ingenuity of that sort of thing is that it immediately classifies him who ventures to disagree, who takes up the cudgels for Poe, as belonging to "a decidedly primitive stage of reflection." As a further specimen of this strange vendetta, consider the paragraph quoted below from James's life of Hawthorne—a remarkable piece of intelligence gone wrong.

> There was but little literary criticism in the United States at the time Hawthorne's earlier works were published; but among the reviewers Edgar Poe perhaps held the scales the highest. He, at any rate, rattled them loudest, and pretended, more than anyone else, to conduct the weighing process on scientific principles. Very remarkable was this process of Edgar Poe's, and very extraordinary were his principles, but he had the advantage of being a man of genius, and his intelligence was frequently great. His collection of critical sketches of the American writers flourishing in what M. Taine would call his milieu and moment, is very curious and interesting reading, and it has one quality which ought to keep it from being ever completely forgotten. It is probably the most complete and exquisite specimen of provincialism ever prepared for the edification of men.

There are two things about this startling paragraph which demand comment. Its first assertion is flatly and demonstrably wrong. *Twice Told Tales* was published in 1837; within a decade of that publication, we have, in the field of criticism, not only Poe, but Emerson, Lowell, Whipple, and Fuller. In the second place, the very process and principles of Poe, at which James sneers so condescendingly, are almost identical at bottom with the process and principles of James himself. Furthermore, the injustice of the whole paragraph is magnified when one considers that Poe comes into the picture because of his review of Hawthorne—the only contemporary review to show anything like understanding and appreciation of Hawthorne's outstanding merit.

It is pleasant to turn from such a piece of perversity to James's study of Maupassant, in which he delivered his matured and final opinion on the matter of art versus morality. To understand the essay fully, one must bear in mind that at the time when James was writing, Maupassant was taboo in English-speaking countries. To watch the intelligence and tact with which the critic handles his delicate subject is a lesson in the practice of criticism. He begins by assuming the moralistic viewpoint, thus gaining the confidence of his moralistic audience. But where ninety-nine English-speaking, and particularly American critics of the day would have proceeded to grow red in the face demanding Maupassant's immediate execution as an offender against public morality, James manages to preserve both his coolness and his sanity.

We are accustomed to think, he remarks, we of the English faith, that a cynic is a living advertisement of his errors. . . . His baseness, as it pervades him, ought to be written all over him; yet somehow there are certain aspects—and those commanding, as the house-agents say—

in which it is not in the least to be perceived. It is easy to exclaim that if he judges life only from the point of view of the senses, many are the noble and exquisite things he must leave out. What he leaves out has no claim to get itself considered till after we have done justice to what he takes in.

And so he proceeds to consider Maupassant's actual accomplishment, paying due tribute to his narrative art, to his style, to his fidelity to those aspects of life he chooses to depict. As to the truth of his realism, James comes to this conclusion:

> No doubt there is in our literature an immense amount of conventional blinking, and it may be questioned whether pessimistic representations in M. de Maupassant's manner do not follow his particular original more closely than our perpetual quest of pleasantness.

After having thus done his author substantial justice, James proceeds to look for his limitation, which he finds to consist in this: that Maupassant unduly simplifies his problem of representing life by leaving out of his picture "the whole reflective part of his men and women—that reflective part which governs conduct and produces character." One may disagree with that conclusion, but one cannot easily call it either stupid or Puritanic.

Finally, at the close of the essay, James breaks into a plea for the freedom of the artist, a plea, in which he rises into an eloquence rare with him.

> Hard and fast rules, a priori restrictions, mere interdictions (you shall not speak of this, you shall not look at that) have surely served their time, and will in the nature of the case never strike an energetic talent as anything but arbitrary. A healthy, living and growing art, full of curiosity and fond of exercise, has an indefeasible mistrust of rigid prohibitions. Let us then leave this magnificent art of the novelist to itself and to its perfect freedom, in the faith that one example is as good as another, and that our fiction will always be decent enough if it be sufficiently general. Let us not be alarmed at this prodigy (though prodigies are alarming) of M. de Maupassant, who is at once so licentious and so impeccable, but gird ourselves up with the conviction that another point of view will yield another perfection.

The fundamental idea of this, that criticism is concerned, not with subject, but with treatment, had been stated, forty years earlier, by James's bête noir, Edgar Poe; its corollaries, that no subject should be forbidden, and that the critic must shift his viewpoint to suit the artist he examines, here make their first appearance in American critical theory; the whole constituting a sort of literary Declaration of Independence.

III

Infinitely varied are the ways in which a man escapes from his native provincialisms. Stedman escaped by way of the classics; James was delivered from the moralistic fallacy by his intense appreciation of technique. With one or two very obscure exceptions, he was the first American critic to treat the novel primarily as a work of art—to consider neither its subject nor its teaching, but its artistic qualities,—form, construction, style, reality. Himself the most conscientious of novelistic technicians, his criticism was pre-eminently technical.[1] Now when a technical master of any art discusses the work of his brother artists in this manner, the result is criticism of the highest interest and value. James discusses Balzac. There is a brief mention of Balzac's life, a word on his personality, a sneer for his philosophy. And then, technicalities—long samples of his descriptions, with an analysis of their function in the novel as a whole; notes on his characterizations, copiously illustrated; searching comments on his dialogue, with extracts. Similar in method is the

[1] Here again, James is like Poe, and like no other preceding American critic.

study of Trollope. Unless one has read Trollope, and read him at length, the essay, with its minute discussion of technical points, is meaningless. Read with proper preparation, it is an invaluable study of the realistic novel in the hands of one of its eminent practitioners.

Technical criticism is both excellent and necessary. Criticism is far too apt to deal in glittering generalities. But criticism that begins and ends with technique gets nowhere. It is also the critic's business to arrive at some sort of reasoned conclusion about his author, to leave us with a clear notion that the author is "placed." And here again, James is not found wanting. He has the gift, one of the supreme gifts of the great critic, of summing up his author in a memorable sentence, rarely dazzling, but never cheap. Of Balzac he says, "Each particular episode of the Comedie Humaine has its own hero and heroine, but the great general protagonist is the twenty-franc piece." And again, "Balzac has that sign of the few supreme geniuses, that if you look long enough, he offers you a specimen of every possible mode of feeling." Trollope is captured in a word. "His great, his inestimable merit was a complete appreciation of the usual." And this, on Gautier, is a masterpiece in miniature.

> His stories are always the measure of an intellectual need to express an ideal of the exquisite in personal beauty and costume, combined with that of a certain serene and full-blown sensuality in conduct, and accompanied with gorgeous visions of upholstery and architecture.

But in spite of his faculty of technical appreciation, and despite his flair for the beautiful in all its forms—a flair that allowed him to be pleased with such a diversity of creatures as Trollope and Stevenson, Zola and Turgeniev, Kipling and George Eliot, there is one pervading fault that mars all of James's criticism on the appreciative side. He was always sensible, civilized in his viewpoint, acute in technical analysis, catholic in taste. But he lacks something of the precious power of enjoyment. He never let himself go, but rather always held himself superior to the artist whose work he examined. When he is handling a subject that calls for satire, as in his essay on George Sand, this superiority gives a delicious result. The study of that lively lady is written throughout with a faintly ironic smile—and that is as it should be. But when we find the critic harping on Hawthorne's provincialism, when we find him cold before *Anna Karénina* and doubtful about *The Ordeal of Richard Feverel*, all is not as it should be. Detachment is no doubt a critical virtue, but like all virtues, it may be carried too far. That same curious timidity and coldness of temperament that froze Henry James for the adventure of life, that whimpers so plaintively through the pages of his letters, operated in his criticism. Enthusiasm for literature he undoubtedly had, but he never surrendered to it; he never bowed the knee in worship before literary greatness. He was too small to become humble; he had always to preserve his superiority by his superciliousness. That is perhaps his chief limitation as a critic.

IV

But acute, balanced, sensible, though unhappily somewhat frigid, as his criticisms of individual authors usually are, criticism of individual authors are not the most important feature of Henry James's critical work. Throughout all these essays, these technical discussions, he was slowly and empirically building up his great critical structure—his theory of the novel.

There was something curiously scientific about James's attitude toward literature. A book was never for him a source of pure delight, a pathway to ecstasy. In one sense, it might be said that he never cared for literature at all. Books, plots, characters, were to him rather pawns in a superb game of chess. He looked at literature, first and last, from the technical side. Like the supreme object of his contempt, Poe, he was constantly curious about the way of the author—curious most of all of his own creative processes. The long series of prefaces to his novels, with their minute and subtle analysis of his methods of production, are the evidence of this. A man does not write that kind of thing unless he is avidly curious about such matters. And when (I repeat) the creative artist of undoubted standing, endowed with such a curiosity, turns to the consideration of his own art, the result is criticism of the highest merit.

Like his friend, ally, and in some respects antithesis, Howells, James was on the surface a prophet of realism. He thought of himself as a realist, and into the cause of realism he poured something of the moral fervor of his Puritan forbears. He was continually insisting that the novel is history, to be taken soberly and seriously by the novelist and the reader. Thus history repeats itself with a difference, and we find James writing a "defence of the novel," just as we earlier found Longfellow and Lowell writing defences of poetry. "It is impossible," James declared, "to imagine what a novelist takes himself to be unless he regards himself as a historian and his narrative as history." [2] Viewing the novel in this light, James was unsparing in his condemnation of all trifling with the seriousness of the art. He sharply rapped Trollope over the knuckles for his habit of remarking in shoulder-shrugging asides that after all this is only a story. The particular thing that drew him to the French novelists of his day, in spite of his reserves, was their whole-souled artistic conscience, their passion for novelistic truth. Thus attached by theory to the realistic school, James naturally viewed with hostility the romantic revival of the nineties, and joined with Howells in that critic's strenuous crusade against the Stevensonians. With justifiable bitterness he exclaimed, "I do hunger and thirst, in this deluge of cheap romanticism and chromolithographic archaisms (babyish, puppyish, as evocation, all, it seems to me) for a note, a gleam of the life *we* live." That, for James, is exceptionally vigorous; more characteristic in expression, though similar in thought, is this: "But we suspect that something even better in a novelist is that tender appreciation of actuality which makes the

[2] Such earnestness is, of course, most praiseworthy, yet it is perhaps a truer sanity that sees in the literary artist more than a little of the circus clown.

application of a single coat of rose-colour seem an act of violence." In such remarks, James was in perfect agreement with Howells in his war for realism. And many of James's literary likings—for Trollope, Flaubert, Eliot, the Russians, were expressions of his love of realism. But there was a great difference between the allies. Howells was consistent. He was the true realist—limited and prudish in practice, though not in theory—but none the less a realist. James was at bottom something far different.

While all of his critical essays are, in some sense, dissertations on the art of the novel, his novelistic creed was most completely expressed in the article called *The Art of Fiction*. In this, which as a discussion of artistic technique deserves to rank with Poe's *Poetic Principle,* we have almost all the virtues of Henry James, free from his irritating critical vices. He begins by stating what is in effect the guiding principle of all his critical writing: "Art lives upon discussion, upon curiosity, upon experiment, upon variety of attempt." Then comes another one of those passages in which he defends his particular art against moralistic depreciators—strange sounding indeed in an age in which the novel is the chief form of literary activity, and reminding us once more that James never quite forgot Boston Common and the Congregational Fathers. Like the old Elizabethan defenders of poetry, James defends the novel on the ground that it is *true*. Standing for a moment on the platform of pure realism, he gravely states, "The only reason for the existence of a novel is that it does attempt to represent life."

But after having begun in this sternly moral and self-denying vein, he suddenly turns about, runs up the red flag, and denounces in anarchistic tones any attempt to limit the freedom of the novelist in any way. "The only obligation," he sweepingly asserts, "to which in advance we may hold a novel, without incurring the accusation of being arbitrary, is that it be interesting." Thus he passes at a step from the moralistic realism of Howells to the nihilism of Cabell. The contradiction is fundamental and irreconcilable, particularly when we add to this statement its further development.

> We must grant the artist his subject, his idea, his donnee; our criticism is applied only to what he makes of it.

Treatment, technique,—if the art of the novelist lies in these things only, what has become of our realistic dogma? The two things are fundamentally opposed. Realism is basically a search for truth. The critic who bases his judgments on a realistic code is perpetually asking, "Are these things true?" He is bound therefore to consider subject matter, even at times to consider it above all else. But the technical critic, the critic who restricts his criticism to the manner of treatment, cannot put that question. What he asks is, "Are these things well done?" His quest, then, is for beauty only. And here, I think, we come close to the secret of Henry James.

Keen as James's intelligence undoubtedly was, much as he gave himself to the practice of meta-critic, minutely as he analyzed his own creative processes, there is no indication that he ever realized this fundamental idealism, or romanticism, in his own temperament. Not that he was without a large realistic element. The realistic element in his make-up is too obvious; indeed, it has misled most critics into calling him a realist pure and simple. But James's realism was largely a matter of principle. His taste told him that the greatest masters of the novel in his day were realists. His residence in France brought him close to such writers as Flaubert, Zola, and above all Turgeniev—men who were not only practicing realists, but theoretical realists as well. Realism was in the air, and from the air he caught it. Furthermore, realism had its appeal to one side of James's temperament—the New England side. Realism is the Puritanism of the novel.

But lying back of this conscientious realism were the genuine and deepest instincts of the man, and these all ran in the opposite direction. Everything about him—criticism, novels, life—points to a timid, half-frustrated, unconfessed, yet intense love of beauty. This is, of course, no new discovery; Stuart Sherman, in an essay which is almost the best study of James yet written, has pointed out the essentially idealistic and beauty-seeking nature of James's novels. But we still go on labelling him realist. However, we are dealing with the master of qualifications, and here again we must qualify. Beauty, as James saw it, was not the rich and sensuous goddess of Gautier and Keats. He was rather enamoured of intellectual beauty—the beauty of deft construction, of subtle artistry, of cultured living, above all, the beauty of a rich and sensitive character. We have but to compare his characters with those of Howells, Marcia Hubbard with Isabel Archer, to perceive the difference between the simon-pure realist and the veiled idealist.

The theory of the novel, like all the theories we have yet examined in this volume, is inconsistent—hopelessly so. And yet, this is no great misfortune.

Literature, like the life it reflects, is too large and varied a thing to be comprehended in any one system—at any rate, in any one system that the human mind has as yet managed to construct. The history of literature is strewn with the wrecks of consistent critical systems—and most of them have ruined their creators as well. Howells, as we shall see, is a case in point. His criticism is consistent; thus it possesses one virtue. James, more intelligent than Howells, more gifted with literary taste, was more fortunate, and his theory allows for, as his appreciation welcomed, both Trollope and Stevenson, Zola and Gautier, Eliot and Kipling. If one were to select, from the considerable mass of American critical writings, half a dozen volumes to be preserved while all the others were destroyed, *Partial Portraits*, would undoubtedly be among the precious half dozen. It is one of the critical masterpieces of all time.

V

Antipathies are often the result of unrealized likenesses; and as we come to sum up Henry James's critical character, we find a number of close resemblances, as we have mentioned in passing, between him and the object of his critical dislike, Poe.

Both, in opposition to the general trend of American criticism, insisted on the separation of art and morals, though both made qualifications of that too absolute dogma. Both possessed, mixed with many elements of "provincialism," that indefinable quality which we call the civilized mind. Both were primarily lovers and critics of technique, and both owned the rare attribute of being able to discuss technique with clearness and precision. And both, attempting to construct critical systems which perhaps fail to hold together as complete systems, have left us generalizations of the greatest value—Poe in the realm of lyric poetry, James in the kingdom of the novel.

In spite of all these resemblances, there is no evidence that James deliberately followed Poe, nor, indeed, any other preceding American critic. His critical masters were rather the French critics of the Nineteenth Century, whom he frequently resembles both in doctrine and in manner. Nevertheless, he was completely in touch with the main critical movements in the America of his day. Indeed, he includes within himself elements of two conflicting schools. In his insistence on technique, in his advocacy of "art for art's sake," he is in complete agreement with Stedman and the critics of the *Cen-*

tury Magazine group. It is interesting in this connection to note that the same basic theory which results, in the Stedman-Aldrich school, in poetry of mere futile prettiness, forms the groundwork, with Henry James, of one of the finest bodies of novels in any literature. On the other hand, as an advocate of realism, as the first consistent advocate of pure realism in American criticism, James is in close touch with critics who stand at the other pole of literary endeavor from the Stedman-Aldrich group. Here, he joins hand with Howells and the literary radicals of the purple nineties. And yet, though James is far superior to Howells as a critic, he had nothing like the immediate effect of Howells. For one thing, he paid no attention whatsoever to the American novels of his day. Furthermore his manner, his very trick of reserve and qualification which makes him the better critic, disqualified him as the leader of a revolt. His criticism never caught the popular ear as did that of Howells. Nevertheless, within a small and select circle, the critical influence of Henry James has been immense. He is the novelist's own critic; wherever, in the English and American novel of the Twentieth Century, one meets a realistic novel of particular excellence, one is apt to find traces of the theory and practice of Henry James.

CRITICAL WRITINGS OF HENRY JAMES

Novels of George Eliot	*Atlantic Monthly,* October, 1866
Lothair	*Atlantic Monthly,* August, 1870
Taine's *English Literature*	*Atlantic Monthly,* April, 1872
French Poets and Novelists	Macmillan, London, 1878
Hawthorne (English Men of Letters)	Harper, New York, 1880
Partial Portraits	Macmillan, New York and London, 1888
Essays in London and Elsewhere	Harper, New York, 1893
Notes on Novelists	Harper, New York, 1914

CHAPTER VII

Howells

I

Contemporary with Stedman and James, with both of whom he maintained personal relations, William Dean Howells was far removed from both of these critics in spirit and in method. While Stedman's criticism casts back longing glances at a type of poetry which the critic knows to be outmoded and dying, Howells boldly faces the future. Like James, he was an advocate of the realistic novel, but unlike James, it was his good fortune to catch the ear of the public. For two stirring decades, from 1890 to 1910, his was easily the most authoritative voice in American criticism. Indeed, one might go farther and assert that of all the American critics we have considered, Howells has been the most directly and immediately influential.

The critical work of Howells falls very distinctly into two periods. The first, from 1866 to 1881, when he was assistant editor and later editor-in-chief of the *Atlantic Monthly,* produced nothing beyond a large number of wholly unimportant reviews, the second, beginning with his occupancy of "The Editor's Study" in *Harper's Magazine* in 1886, lasted until his death in 1920. Thus, by the simple expedient of outlasting all his contemporaries, Howells became, as Lowell had done before him, the dean of American letters. But Howells's deanship, unlike Lowell's, was no mere honorary distinction. While Lowell, as age crept on, withdrew more and more from the living currents of literature, and became eventually only an august name, Howells remained, almost to the day of his death, a moving force in contemporary letters.

In his critical theories, Howells was at once the last of the New Englanders and the first of the moderns. There is still something pathetically humorous in the profound reverence he exhibited for the old tradition, for the literary lights of Boston, for the sacred soil of New England, even while he was preaching, with all his heart and soul, the worship of a new god.

II

Like the oldest New England critics, Howells believed in the union of art and morals. The general tendency, from 1815 on, had been to separate these warring elements; in the criticism of Stedman and James, the divorce is almost complete. Now, Howells suddenly reverses the process, and enunciates firmly that art should teach, not only morality, but Puritan morality. That there can be such a thing as the unmoral in art he calls a "metaphysical lie." Entertaining indeed is Howells's attitude toward that apotheosis of the unmoral in art—Falstaff. The voice of centuries tells him that Falstaff is one of the great characters of literature. He feels as though he ought to admire Falstaff; he really tries hard to do so, but he can't. He is both relieved and delighted when Shakespeare finally dismisses the old reprobate into oblivion. Thus Shakespeare is justified and morality is preserved.

Along with this Puritanical love of high morality went the Puritanical contempt for beauty. It seems a little incongruous to hear one of the masters of English prose—a writer whose most constant excellence is the smooth and fluid beauty of his style—declaring that "it is not noble to love the beautiful, or to live for it, or only by it; and it may not even be refining." Walter Pater preaching in a whitewashed chapel on the doctrine of original sin, Praise-God Barebones writing sonnets to his lady's eyebrow—these would hardly be greater incongruities. No doubt Howells said more than he meant, and the reason for the overstatement is plain to be seen. During the seventies and eighties, Art for Art's Sake had had its day, and had produced, on the whole, nothing of value. And just as Stedman had revolted from the bleakness of Puritanic critical theory, so Howells was now revolting from the emptiness of the art-school.

Howells's depreciation of beauty in literature arose from a desire to emphasize more strongly what he considered the highest quality of a work of art—its truth. As to the relation between truth and beauty, his conception was by no means clear. At one point he saw them as antitheses; at another he viewed truth as an essential part of beauty. And by truth he meant, not truth in the Keatsian sense, not poetic or idealized truth, but genuine, hard, concrete fact, unadorned, unarranged. To the commoner passions of human nature—hatred, ambition, sexual craving—Howells always seemed a bit insensible. As John Macy, in his acute, though highly adverse criticism, has pointed out, the lack of passion is the great defect of Howells's novels. Macy attributes this to the lack of passion in the writer's own temperament. But we cannot hope to understand and appreciate the man unless we recognize that, cool though he may have been in other respects, his mind was warmed by one great passion—the passion for truth.

This passion for truth was the foundation-stone of his theory of the novel—the theme of nearly all his criticism. In his love for truth—not mere abstract truth, but facts, reality—he became lyric. "Ah, poor real life, which I love," he chanted, "can I make others share the delight I feel in thy foolish and insipid face?" The great virtue of the novel, then, is its truth; it should present the facts of life just as they occur. From this basic theory, and its logical corollaries, Howells judges all novelists. And unlike most critics, he applied his logical theory with logical rigor. There are no exceptions, mere taste is allowed no voice in the judgment. Characterization should be rounded, life-like, without either simplification or idealization; therefore down with Dickens. The novelist should never disturb our sense of actuality by an intrusion of his personality; hang Thackeray! Real life has neither beginning, middle, nor end; neither should the novel. "The greatest achievements of fiction, in its highest sense, is to present a picture of life; and the deeper the sense of something desultory, unfinished, imperfect it gives, even in the region of conduct, the more admirable it seems." In strict accordance with this theory, he finds one of the chief excellences of Henry James to consist in the fact that James always draws a character from the outside; that we seldom know in his novels the exact motives of a character, just as we are usually in the dark regarding the motives of the men we meet in life; that he leaves us to form our own conclusions about his personages, neither gilding nor blackening, just as we must form our own judgments of people in the world.

With this extraordinarily rigid and narrow code of laws for the novel spread open on his judicial bench, Howells summoned into court all the array of great novelists, past and present, and judged them all by the strict letter of the law. Beside the tremendous iconoclasm of this performance, the daring flights of the Menckenian school are as nothing. Thus he summarized the "advance" of the English novel. "The art of fiction, as Jane Austen knew it, declined from her through Scott and Bulwer, and Dickens, and Charlotte Brontë, and Thackeray, and even George Eliot." In that strangely misnamed book, *My Literary Passions*—it should be *My Literary Disillusionments*—the hanging judge is everywhere present. Reade, Macaulay, Pope, Chaucer, Fielding, Molière, Balzac, even Flaubert and Turgeniev, are damned as artistically imperfect. Jeffrey could do no more.

III

So far, we have viewed Howells as a consistent realist. In his advocacy of pure reality, of complex characterization, of formless plots, of auctorial impersonality, he was a modern of the moderns, pointing forward ten, twenty, thirty years to the work of Dreiser, Lawrence, and Anderson. But in one important respect he stood at the opposite pole from these men. If there is one privilege that the modern realist claims above all others, it is that of free, plain, and not infrequently coarse speech on any topic under heaven with which he wishes to deal. Such a position as that, though thoroughly in accord with Howells's basic doctrine of the novel, was utterly inacceptable to one of his Puritanic rearing and super-refined temperament. He was, at bottom, a prude; beyond all other writers of anything like his size, beyond all other critics of equal eminence, a prude. There is an amusing passage in *Literary Friends and Acquaintance,* in which he relates, with shrinking squeamishness, how Lowell, wishing to express his sense of the superlative beauty of Dante, did so by the vulgar expletive "Damn." We have already noted his disapproval of Falstaff. In the same spirit he went through the whole classic canon, blue-penciling all passages unfit for a Sunday-school library. Chaucer, Fielding, Cervantes —no one is too high to be reached by this condemnation. His whole attitude toward classic literature might be summed up in the sentence: "The worst of the literature of past times, before an ethical conscience began to inform it, is that it leaves the mind fouled with filthy images and base thoughts."

One other curious reserve of Howells remains to be noted. Relatively passionless in life, quite passionless in his novels, he was equally passionless in his theory of the novel. The novel, he thought, should not depict scenes of strong passion; not because such scenes are unreal, but because they are indelicate exhibitions, and if not positively distressing, at least ought to be so, in the eyes of the female reader for whom the modern novel is written.

IV

Considered in the absolute, whether as a body of literary theory or as a collection of judgments of individual authors, the criticism of Howells is bad—

there is no other word for it. A criticism that can find, among all the authors it meets—and Howells was a wide reader—only three—Jane Austen, Anthony Trollope, and Leo Tolstoy—who are deserving of any large measure of praise, has plainly gone wrong somewhere.[1] Part of the difficulty, of course, lies in the fact that Howells had a theory and stuck to it. Most critics have theories, which are quietly discarded when they get in the critic's way. And one must reluctantly admire the courage and consistency of Howells the man, even while one condemns Howells the critic.

But it is perhaps better not to judge Howells the critic in the absolute. His criticism is not food, but physic, useful only in time of sickness. And his was a time of sickness. To understand that sickness, one must thumb through the old files of *Harper's*, of the vintage of 1900. Seen in its proper setting, surrounded by the historical-romantical soothing syrup of Justus Miles Forman, by the early potboilers of James Branch Cabell, by the Wardour Street dialogue of Mary Johnston, by the senti-

[1] Perhaps I too overstate. Howells does not condemn without qualification. He sees excellence in all the great authors whom he considers. But the final impression, and this is what counts in criticism, is one of general condemnation. Note how Howells, in his narrow doctrine and his general aversion from authors of the past, approaches the critics of the 18th Century.

mental drool and drivel of a dozen others, this criticism of Howells's begins to take on meaning.

Howells the novelist, and to a far greater extent Howells the critic, was a literary radical—the great literary radical of his age and country. It was the Indian summer of romanticism, the great age of the historical novel. Stanley Weyman was turning out volume after volume, ready made according to the cloak-and-sword formula; Winston Churchill was serving up dilute extract of *The Virginians;* lesser men did far worse. Realism, never too hospitably received in America, momentarily triumphant in the seventies and early eighties, was suddenly swamped by the flood of the New Romance. From all this Howells revolted. His critical merits and his critical defects were largely the result of this revolt. A realist by taste and tradition, the first thorough-going and fundamental realist in American criticism, he saw clearly that the great fault in American literature of the day lay in the fact that the American author had lost his grip on reality; that he was working in a realm of cheap and conventional fantasy. Novels were no longer imitations of life, but imitations of imitations of imitations. The remedy, according to Howells, was to turn away from models, to drop all conventions of art, to cease trying to be artistic, and to reproduce life itself—pure, unadulterated life. Part of this, of course, has been the cry of literary reformers in all ages. "Back to Nature" has been the watchword of every literary school for the past four hundred years. But with Howells the old cry took on a new significance; it became no mere meaningless platitude, but a demand for facts. This was an idea that the age had forgotten. It needed to be stated, to be repeated; and for years Howells hammered away at it, damning the romanticist, praising all evidences of realism, until at last he saw realism triumphant.

Unfortunately, the heat of controversy proved too much for Howells's judgment. He began by condemning the fundamental error in post-Stevensonian romanticism; he ended by denying that some of its merits were merits. The only explanation for some of the queer quirks of theory in which he sometimes indulges is that after so long a fight against romanticism, he had at last come to believe that whatever was opposite to romantic practice must be right. The strongest feature of the romantic novel was its plot. The characters might be wooden, the dialogue stilted, the incidents unnatural, but a well-built plot there had to be. Howells, the revolutionary, went, like all revolutionaries, to the other extreme; there ought to be no plot. The post-Stevensonian romanticist summarily classified his characters as hero and villain. Howells, revolting, declared that the novelist should assume an attitude of utter impartiality, leaving decision to the reader. The romanticist delighted in a highly conclusive ending. We may not like his typical together-forever last chapter, but we must admit that it is, in the novelistic sense, final. Howells, reacting, cried that the novel should have no conclusion, should merely stop. Perhaps even his dislike of passion in the novel was due not only to his temperament, but also to the fact that the theme of ninety-nine romantic novels out of a hundred is passionate love. In all these doctrines, Howells perhaps went too far. At least, he seems to have made no attempt to conform his practice to his theory. He built his plots, classified his characters, commented on the action through character-mouthpieces, and rounded off his endings with commendable nicety. But while these excesses of theory certainly hurt his work as judicial criticism, they increase its effectiveness as a preachment. In order to free itself completely from romantic convention, the novel had to err in the opposite direction.

But the services of Howells to literary criticism

did not stop at the negative task of attacking decadent romanticism. Unlike so many critics of weight, who, when they grow old, withdraw to the quiet of their libraries, and spend their twilight years in meditating over days gone by, Howells remained to the end the most receptive of critics. Secure in position, too old to feel jealousy, benevolent by temperament, it was his pleasure to welcome and assist every young realist of promise who appeared during his critical reign.

His chief discovery, perhaps, was Frank Norris, whom he hailed as the greatest American novelist of his generation. Howells had a genuine literary passion for Norris, and his repeated expression of that passion has had a great deal to do with Norris's posthumous reputation. More surprising was his recognition of Stephen Crane, from whom he differed as widely as two realists can differ in temperament and in principles. Howells was the first critic of importance to take George Ade seriously; he was an early admirer of Ernest Poole, of Edith Wharton, of Booth Tarkington. Here, Howells is unlike most critics, who are apt to be indulgent to dead authors and severe with live ones. For dead classics, Howells has little respect unless they measure up to his rather narrow standard. Toward living writers—romanticists excluded—his benevolence far exceeds his power of discrimination. Thus we find him praising, along with Norris and Crane, and with no apparent sense of a difference in literary stature, Edith Wyatt and Kathleen Norris and Brand Whitlock. The praise he accords Whitlock would not be unworthy of a Galsworthy or a Hardy.

Nor was this receptivity confined to American novelists only. Firmly rooted to the soil, thoroughly American in idea and in temperament, Howells had nevertheless more of the international viewpoint than any critic we have so far examined. The name of Henry James will at once occur to every reader; but James's internationalism was sharply restricted by his absolute indifference to American literature. Howells achieved the charming combination of literary patriotism and literary internationalism. His cult of the Russians, particularly Tolstoy, has already been mentioned; to him is largely due their acceptance by the American public. Manzoni, Valdes, Auerbach, Arnold Bennett, Björnson, Zola, Galdos, Erckmann-Chatrian—such a list is cosmopolitan enough to satisfy the most exacting taste. Howells realized that not only are the classics international, but that speed of communication has made modern literature also international; the literary movement that started in Rome yesterday will be in New York tomorrow, and in Chicago the day after.

Not only was Howells the first American critic to give himself up whole-heartedly to realism; in one other respect, at least, his work diverges sharply from that which just preceded it. In the chapter on Stedman we have noted how the late romantic poets, turning from the corruption and vulgarity of the Gilded Age, deliberately divorced the literature they were attempting to produce from the life they saw about them. This attitude of withdrawal was shared by perhaps a majority of the American writers of the seventies and eighties; thus Lowell shut himself up in his study; James and Harte fled to England; Crawford sought beauty in Rome; and Burroughs and Miller retired to the solitude of nature. Howells, realist because he actually loved life, stayed on in the thick of the press, stayed on to see, in the late eighties and early nineties, amid the roar of Pullman strikes and the shouts of the Populists, the dawn of a new day.

Viewed in the clearest light, the whole realistic movement sponsored by Howells might be considered merely a part of the general awakening of the American civic conscience which took place during the time when Howells occupied the pulpit in *Harper's.* The connection between the realistic novel of Howells and his allies and the reform movement has not, I think, been clearly traced; it exists, none the less. Before the reform comes always the exposé, and the realistic novel, by putting down the facts of life just as it sees them, in all their undisguised ugliness, constitutes the most effective and far-reaching type of exposé. This is not strongly evident in the novels of Howells himself; he avoided too sedulously the scandalous and the unpleasant, though even in his later novels there is an undercurrent of dissatisfaction with the world as he found it. In his *Easy Chair* papers, however, the reform motive is a leading one; side by side with favorable criticisms of Norris and Crane we find attacks on various phases of social evil. And in the work of his allies, we get the reform impulse in full blast. *The Octopus* is a more effective attack on the great corporations of the day than *The History of the Standard Oil; Main-Travelled Roads* is as Populistic as a speech of Bryan's. Stephen Crane doubtless never thought himself a reformer, but *Maggie* showed up the evils of the slums as well as any article by Jacob Riis. One might go on multiplying illustrations by the page; the fact is evident. In the nineties, American literature, and with it American criticism of literature, was once more coming to grips with American life, and a large share of the glory of this falls to Howells.

V

Around Howells gathered a whole group of critics, the most definite and unified group since the early days of the *North American*. Two older men belonged to this group—Charles Dudley Warner and George William Curtis. Curtis's critical writings are not of themselves highly important. He is remembered rather as the archetype, in this period, of the literary man turned political and social reformer. Warner wrote more criticism, in which in general his viewpoint is the strictly realistic. Unlike Howells, however, he did not attain perfect consistency. Thus, in 1895 we find him declaring that so unrealistic a work as *Trilby* was the greatest novel of the decade.

But far more important in the movement than these old veterans were the young men—the genuine radicals of the nineties. Foremost of these was Frank Norris. There is significance in the very title of Norris's one critical book—*The Responsibilities of the Novelist*—indicating as it does the evangelical seriousness with which these men took their fiction. In this volume Norris began by asserting that "today is the day of the novel"; that the novel had become the chief form of literary art. Furthermore he noted, that whereas literature had formerly been the playground of the cultured few, democracy and the extension of literacy had made it food for the multitude. From these facts comes the responsibility of the novelist. Let him express it in his own words.

> How necessary it becomes, for those who, by the simple art of writing, can invade the heart's heart of thousands, whose novels are received with such measureless earnestness—how necessary it becomes for those who wield such power to use it rightfully.

The novelist, then, has a duty, and his chief duty, as Norris saw it, was to tell the truth. But Norris clearly recognized, as few critics before him had recognized, that telling the truth is something more than mere photographic realism. While the theoretically perfect realist, the writer who merely presents facts with absolute detachment, without taking sides or drawing conclusions, does exist, he is a rare bird indeed. Nine-tenths of the novelists ordinarily classed as realists do have an ulterior motive—a thesis to defend, an idea to present. This to Norris was no defect. He boldly defended the novel with a purpose—a purpose of telling things and of showing things. This, of course, demands form, selection, arrangement; and here Norris parted company with Howells, who thought that the novel should have none of these things.

In fact, while the general direction of Norris's criticism was undoubtedly realistic, he refused to class himself as a realist. He preferred to call himself a romancer, though his definition of romance leaves room for any number of realistic elements to creep in.

> Romance is the kind of fiction that takes cognizance of variations from the type of normal life. Realism is the kind of fiction that confines itself to the type of normal life.

The trouble with a definition of that kind is that it makes no distinctions. There is no novel written that does not contain variations from the type of normal life. All novels, therefore are romantic, and romance and realism becomes perfectly meaningless terms. But though the definition is worthless in itself, it is interesting to us as showing Norris's attempt to escape from the prison-house of Howellsian realism. Unlike Howells, Norris had no quarrel with the historical novel per se; but the historical novel of his own day, the historical novel become a convention and a fashion, he handled as severely as Howells had done.

But Norris's powers as a critic are best demonstrated by two ideas which stand somewhat outside the main thesis of his volume. The first of these was his discovery of the frontier as a chief "matter" of American literature. The thing itself was old enough; even before Cooper the frontier was furnishing American literature with one of its principal themes. But it was Norris who first labeled and ticketed the frontier in American literature, who traced its various developments from Cooper to Garland, and who noted that in his own day the frontier was no more. Thus in an essay he anticipated the chief notions of several of last year's ponderous and scholarly tomes.

The second idea, Norris's main contribution to the theory of the novel, has not had, I think, the attention it deserves. Having discarded, to all intents, the old distinction between romantic and realistic novelists, Norris proceeded to divide writers of fiction into two new classes—novelists and storytellers. By novelist he means the depictor of character, the purveyor of ideas, the conscious artist, who mixes his colors with brains. Over against him, Norris sets the story-teller, pure and simple, the man who has but one talent, that of relating a string of incidents with such power that the reader is held in thrall. The greatest fiction writers, Norris thought, included in themselves both these characters. In lesser men, they often exist in complete disjunction; and as types of his antithesis, Norris cleverly selects Tolstoy, great novelist and bad story teller, and Conan Doyle, story teller in the highest degree—and nothing else. This bit of insight alone marks out Norris as potentially a great critic. Unfortunately, this one volume is all he has left us in that kind.

VI

His co-worker, Hamlin Garland, was at once a far better Howellsian and a far inferior critic. One hesitates at first to attribute such a piece of critical nonsense as *Crumbling Idols* to the author of *Main Travelled Roads*—until one remembers that this is also the author of that perfect western-movie scenario, *The Captain of the Gray Horse Troop*. *Crumbling Idols* has all the unbridled enthusiasm, and all the mental weakness of a religious tract.

There is for Garland but one kind of novel, to which he attaches the pompous and question-begging label, "veritism." From this bad beginning, Garland goes on to evolve a strange mixture of a priorism and prophecy. "Veritism," he declares, "puts aside all models." Writers have been announcing, for the past two thousand years, that now they are going to put aside all models and return to nature; so far as my limited reading informs me, no one has done it yet. The great vice of American literature, Garland concluded—with some reason—was lack of provincialism. The fiction of the future, in his view, must be local fiction. But—and here he goes far off the track—good local fiction can be produced only by a native of the locality. He digs up the hoary old fallacy of the earliest American critics, a fallacy laughed out of existence by Lowell fifty years before, that a great countryside produces literature by a sort of auto-generation. Thus, California is bound to be the mother of a great literature. This brings us to what one might call Garland's literary populism. He believed, like Emerson, that America began at the Alleghanies, and that American literature in the truest sense could never be produced in the Europe-worshipping cities of the Atlantic seaboard. Boston as a literary center is dead; New York is doomed; American literature in the future will come from Kalamazoo and Gopher Prairie. To this collection of critical mare's nests, Garland adds another—the pseudo-sociological. The literature of the past, he announces, was feudalistic; that of the future must be democratic. This idea was new, I believe with Garland; it has since done duty pretty often. We even had the other day a volume entitled *The Sociological Criticism of Literature*. I have met a fair number of types of criticism. I think I know what aesthetic criticism means, and technical criticism, and impressionistic, and judicial, and historical, and even expressionistic, but I confess that sociological criticism still remains one of the great sealed mysteries.

Amid all these prophecies, one only hits the mark. Garland did foresee that the novel of the immediate future would consist very largely of destructive criticism of American life; but this is one hit among twenty misses. As criticism, this volume is almost worthless; as a symptom, it is invaluable. It lands us in the full tide of dogmatic and uncompromising realism. For thirty years afterward, orthodox criticism of the novel did little more than repeat Howells and Norris and Garland.

CRITICAL WORKS OF WILLIAM DEAN HOWELLS

Criticism and Fiction — Harper, New York, 1891
My Literary Passions — Harper, New York, 1895
Heroines of Fiction, 2 vols. — Harper, New York, 1901
Literary Friends and Acquaintance — Harper, New York, 1900
Literature and Life — Harper, New York, 1902
My Mark Twain — Harper, New York, 1910

Howells contributed a great number of reviews to *The Atlantic Monthly* between 1866 and 1880. More significant are his contributions to *Harper's Magazine*, in "The Editor's Study" from 1885 to 1892, in "The Easy Chair" from 1900 to 1920.

FOLLOWERS OF HOWELLS

Hamlin Garland, *Crumbling Idols*, 1893.
Frank Norris, *The Responsibilities of the Novelist*, Doubleday, Page, New York, 1903.

CHAPTER VIII

HUNEKER

I

EVERY now and then some criticaster, of the sort who believe that authors can be ranked and graded like pupils in a class in elementary arithmetic, sets out to answer the question, Who is the great American critic? The answers to this question have been various and surprising. Lowell has been most often mentioned, but one also hears the names of Poe, Stedman, and even Margaret Fuller. No one, however, has as yet nominated for the honor James Huneker. Indeed, of all the major American critics, Huneker has been most persistently ignored. The qualities of the man are so obvious that this demands some attempt at explanation. This neglect is no doubt partly due to his lifelong connection with the daily papers—a connection that invites the academic epithet—journalistic. More of it is owing to Huneker's critical isolation. Most critics, the reader has probably noticed, speak not only for themselves, but for some group of creative writers, or some general movement of literary thought. They are party leaders, and the party helps them to fame. But Huneker belonged to no movement, advocated no reform, was touted by no clique, and it has been in the interest of no particular literary group to shout his praises. Only abroad has his importance been recognized. Remy de Gourmont, Paul Bourget, George Brandes, men whose mere awareness of the existence of an American critic meant a great deal, recorded their estimation of him in flattering terms. Nor was this undeserved. One can give him no higher praise that to say that in range of interests, in keenness of intelligence, in catholicity of taste, in brilliance of style, he reminds one constantly of the great French critics of the Nineteenth Century, of Sainte-Beuve and Taine and Le Maître.

II

He is a fascinating subject of study. All great critics are personalities; few are as interesting, as pleasing, as personal as Huneker. His essays tell us a great deal about the men he criticized, and still more about James Huneker. Every line of his prose rings with the accent of a living human voice. Every opinion he utters is of interest, not only because it is or is not true, but because he utters it. And to understand and appreciate his criticism, one must know something of the life he lived, the circumstances that shaped him, the forces that made him what he was.

James Gibbons Huneker was born in Philadelphia in 1860. His ancestry was largely Irish; his family name probably of remote Hungarian origin. His father was a well-to-do business man, who in his off hours collected etchings, haunted the theatre and the concert hall, drank brandy with Poe, and entertained at his house Thalberg and Ole Bull. The boy grew up in an atmosphere of unacademic culture. Books and music and pictures came to him, not as a discovery of late adolescence, tinged with a flavor of exoticism, but as a natural and almost essential part of everyday life. He was equally at home in Bohemia and in Belgravia.

He was brought up in the Roman Catholic Church. It may seem fantastic to connect Huneker's theological training with his qualities as a literary critic, but such a connection nevertheless exists. Tolerance, catholicity, freedom from excessive moralism, are among the most desirable of qualities in a critic. Now not one person in ten thousand, Protestant born and reared, ever escapes from the overshadowing influence of Puritanism. The literary critic born a Protestant who remains orthodox, is bound to disapprove of some of the greatest things in literature; and even though he rids himself of his dogmas in theology, he finds it almost impossible to escape them in morals. Thence comes the critical prudery that so defaces the work of Howells; even such liberals as Stedman and Lowell are restricted by it, and we find Stedman averse to Poe, and Lowell looking with disapproval at Fielding and Whitman. In lesser men than these, Puritanism leads to the oddities that make the early issues of the *North American Review* sound so often like a critical joke book.

These are the conservatives, the comparatively orthodox. The heretics are apt to be equally biased, though in a different direction. The critic brought up under Protestantism and Puritanism who revolts violently against the religion of his forbears becomes, in ninety-nine cases out of a hundred, a violent and partisan anti-moralist. In either case the results are bad. The orthodox Puritan is blind to the shining glories of Rabelais, Cabell, and large parts of Chaucer and Shakespeare. The anti-Puritan, who is only a Puritan facing the other way, can often see no good in Emerson and Hawthorne and Tennyson.

From the one-sided excesses of both these groups the Catholic training of Huneker helped to preserve him. Vague though the liberal Catholic may become in doctrine, he retains to the end something of the religious emotion, some not-too-sharply defined theological base, some moral taste, from the safe ground of which he can view with tolerance and curiosity those whose notions do not strictly coincide with his own. Thus Huneker, never having felt the pressure of Puritanism, never felt it necessary to indulge in anti-Puritan rages. He listened with detached and intelligent interest to the sermons of literary moralists like Shaw and Ibsen. He recognized the moral instinct in human nature, and examined with curiosity and sympathy its literary manifestations. But unlike the Puritan, he never expected too much of human nature. He knew that even the saints have their days off, and he was not above a human pleasure in the contemplation of these worthies in their moments of weakness. Ribaldry—a liking for an earthy tale—is one element of the complete man; therefore we have a literature of ribaldry. Both the Puritan, who shrieks "Wipe it out," and the anti-Puritan, who demands it everywhere and then attempts to prove that it does not exist, are untrue to the facts of literature and life. Huneker did neither; he was neither prudish nor prurient. He dealt with many authors who were under the moral ban—Wedekind, George Moore, d'Annunzio—but without descending to become either an apologist or a censor. The point is worth emphasizing, because this detachment, this balance, this moral tolerance, has been sadly lacking in most of our American critics.

In 1878 Huneker, having completed his very sketchy formal education, passed a desultory year or two in a law office, and concluding at length that music was his vocation, set out for Paris to complete his musical education. The results of this foreign sojourn, coming during the formative years of Huneker's life, were greatly beneficial. It was this early visit abroad that made him the most cosmopolitan of American critics. There is, of course, an element of cosmopolitanism in nearly every great critic—some second field to which he can turn, and from which he can draw comparisons with the literature of his own time and country. With Lowell it is the Middle Ages, with Stedman the Greeks, with James the French realists, with Howells the Russians. Poe is the only exception in American criticism to this rule—but Poe is an exception to all rules. Huneker, however, was cosmopolitan in a far more thoroughgoing manner than any of these men. He was at home in more lands and literatures than any other American critic.

These earliest wanderyears brought him into close contact with French literature at a time when French literature was in one of its most productive phases—at a time when its character was such as to make its influence particularly tonic on a student from America. Victor Hugo was at the height of his glory. Flaubert and Maupassant might be seen in the cafés. Zola was preaching naturalism and writing his peculiar brand of romanticism. The young musician, already a reader of Baudelaire, Stendhal, and Chateaubriand, soaked himself to saturation in the French writers of the day; from that time on, French was as natural to him as English. A constant journeying back and forth across the Atlantic kept this cosmopolitan sense alive in Huneker to the end. Thus he runs up to Christiania to interview Ibsen; spends a week-end in Kent with Conrad; argues realism with Huysmans, and Shakespeare with Maeterlinck. By such personal contacts Huneker remained always in touch with literature in the making all over Europe. And yet, unlike that other literary cosmopolitan, Henry James, he never became in any sense an expatriate, but remained to the end as American as fried chicken.

Aside from his knowledge of French literature, Huneker learned two facts of importance during his stay in Paris—that he could never become a musician worth listening to, and that he could write things for which editors were willing to pay. As a result of this enlightenment, Huneker, on his return to America, plunged into journalism, first as music critic, later as critic of literature, drama, and painting, for half a dozen New York papers. His letters are a half-comic, half-tragic record of the constant struggle to grind out his daily grist; he wrote with the printer's devil at his elbow. To some men, such a pressure to write much and rapidly would have been fatal. No doubt Huneker did turn out a great deal of criticism of no permanent value. Fortunately, however, he possessed the faculty of self-criticism. The trivial and the ephemeral in his work is safely buried in the files of the *Sun,* the *Times,* the *Herald,* where only the inordinately curious need disturb it. The fifteen volumes which he thought worthy of an appearance in book form are of as uniform and high a quality as those of the most cloistered recluse in critical history. For one thing, this journalistic effort kept him thoroughly alive—if indeed a man of such abounding vitality and such inexhaustible curiosity needed any outside influence to keep him alive—to the literary currents of his day, preventing that ossification of interest which so often overtakes critics as they pass middle age. And it strengthened his impulse to write criticism that is readable and brilliant. This brilliance, this verbal cleverness does, it is true, at times degenerate into cheapness, but it is not the cheapness of the jaded humorist. Huneker never sounds tired; his cheapness resembles rather the occasional cheapness of Dickens and Shakespeare. It is the result of a creative vitality that refused to submit to the slow patient methods of Flaubert and James.

III

Such were the influences that formed him. But what of the man himself, the personality on which these influences worked? The one great quality that irradiates every page of Huneker's criticism is his superb vitality. We are most of us such bloodless creatures that the spectacle of a literary critic so thoroughly alive at once astounds and inspires. He never exhibited a sign of mental fatigue; his spirit never drooped. His curiosity was boundless. His detachment was far removed from the bored aloofness of the typical academic critic. It was rather due to the feeling that there are so many interesting things in life that one cannot properly limit himself to any one group of interests, to any one kind of excellence. Full-blooded as few critics are, he liked best that literature which is rich in personality, teeming with life and passion. Furthermore, this personality of Huneker's spread itself at large in his writing. Such an air of high enjoyment exhales from the page that it takes possession of the reader. One is constantly, in reading Huneker, seized with a desire to go straight from the critic to the author criticized. This quality, which we find also in Lowell, is one of the rarest qualities of the great critic.

Most critics of strong vitality become leaders of movements, literary propagandists. It was Huneker's peculiar excellence to combine liveliness with detachment. An intense individualist, he abhorred movements, reforms, the uplift in all its manifestations, not because of any anti-moralistic bias, but because he hated all attempts to regiment humanity, to standardize, to take from the individual his liberty to develop his peculiarities at his own sweet will. It was his intense individualism, his dislike of the crowd, that drew Huneker to Ibsen. Ibsen was of all modern writers the one with whose philosophy Huneker was in closest agreement.

To class men, without qualifications of all sorts, as optimists or pessimists, is a silly proceeding. Temperamentally, Huneker was an optimist in the sense that, enjoying life vastly, he approved of life. But he was something more than a stomach ambulatory. His keen and searching, naturally undogmatic, restless, questioning intellect, fed on such writers as Flaubert, Conrad, Nietzsche, inevitably turned toward skeptical pessimism. Instinctively, as he admits, a yes-sayer, his mind penetrated easily the fallacies of vulgar American optimism. But although he seemed at times to doubt all things, he never appeared tortured by his doubts. Skepticism in him merely produced a wider tolerance, a greater range of vision. It gave a needed spice of sharpness to his general good nature. He even had his flashes of nihilism; he enjoyed profound pessimism, as he found it in the pages of Gorky and Strindberg. Huneker understood himself pretty thoroughly;

with characteristic frankness he summed himself up in this fashion:

> I am an optimist at bottom, with a superficial coating of pessimism, which thaws near a piano, a pretty girl, or a glass of Pilsner.

A second quality combines with this purely intellectual pessimism to temper a vitality that might otherwise have become mere vigorous barbarism. It is a curious and unquestionable fact, that for all his healthy enjoyment of the world, Huneker was in some sense a mystic. Through all his Bohemian years, he was always keenly sensitive to the beauty of religion. "I love," he declared, "the odour of incense, the mystic bells, the music, the atmosphere of the altar, above all the intellectual life of the church." Frequently one may detect a critic's profoundest likings, not by the author with whom he avowedly deals, but by those whom he incidentally quotes; it is often these who lie deepest imbedded in his consciousness. Thus one may test the sincerity of Huneker's interest in the intellectual life of the church by the fact that he was constantly, in all manner of contexts, quoting Newman. It is this mystic strain which accounts for Huneker's great, perhaps exaggerated liking for Maeterlinck; and we even find him plunging into the mystic reveries of St. John of the Cross.

To the business of criticism Huneker brought, besides his magnificent personality, one of the finest critical equipments in literary history. He was by far the most versatile of American critics—one of the most versatile of all critics. Not only did he range from English and American literature to French, German, Scandinavian, Russian; literature itself was not wide enough to confine his exploring mind. Indeed, it is questionable whether literary criticism was after all his chief interest, whether his achievements in that quarter constitute his largest claim to remembrance. Music was his first love, and perhaps at all times his deepest. His first published volumes bore the title *Mezzotints in Modern Music*. His work on Chopin, which appeared in 1900, really established him as a writer. So important an element in his personality were his musical tastes, that it is worth while to glance at them for a moment. He began as a romanticist; his taste was formed in the seventies and eighties; his prime favorite in music was always Chopin. Liszt he estimated more highly than do most musical critics.

Strauss he regarded as the greatest of contemporary composers. Wagner fascinated him. One of his best essays in musical criticism was devoted to Tschaikovsky. But for popular and sentimental romanticism—the romanticism of Mendelssohn, Massenet, Meyerbeer—he had no use. He thought little of the more popular works of Chopin—the Nocturnes and most of the Valses. But a musical romanticist he in essence remained; a romanticist, however, with strong classical leanings. For the earlier and simpler classics, Mozart, Haydn, Gluck, he had little taste, comparatively speaking. They lacked the idiosyncrasy, the emotional stir, the dissonant element, which appealed to Huneker in music as in literature. But there is a profoundly classical base in any man who "begins his mornings with Bach." And Huneker's condemnation of opera,

> We would rather listen to a Beethoven string quartet played by the Flonzaleys than to all the operas ever written; the majority of them depicting soul states in a sanatorium.

is profoundly classical in its implications. And then, with the characteristic indifference of the great critic to logical consistency, he went to the opera, went and recorded with delight his reactions there.

It is interesting to note his attitude toward such moderns as Schoenberg. He was at first repelled by Schoenberg, found him incomprehensible. But characteristically, he did not turn away with the usual remark that this was not music. He listened, puzzled, but curious, and finally managed to make something of the composer, though arriving at no great liking of him.

His method in musical criticism showed this same mixture of classic and romantic elements. He was always interested in the personality of the composer; this is, I suppose, a form of romanticism. He attempted to capture and express in words the emotional content of the music he discussed. But unlike the so-called literary critic of music, he never wrote programmes. His was a musical criticism for musicians, not for weak-minded amateurs who insist that music should tell them a story. His criticism of music, like Poe's criticism of literature, was highly, almost overpoweringly technical. To understand the last half of his volume on Chopin, one must read with an open score at hand; otherwise, the book is incomprehensible. It is an interesting comment on the direction of technical criticism that Huneker's criticism of music is far more technical than his criticism of literature, and that his condemnations of composers are ten times as numerous, and twenty times as absolute, as his condemnations of authors.

One finds the same qualities in his work as a critic of painting—wide knowledge, classical backbone, liking for the new, the exotic, the strange. His three idols in painting were Vermeer, Velasquez, and Rembrandt. But he was among the first in America to praise the work of Gauguin, and his pages are filled with reference to such men as Monticelli, Piranesi, Felicien Rops.

In characteristic and illuminating phrase, he labelled himself "Jack of the Seven Arts." In one issue of the *Sun* he published articles on Botticelli, on Rodin, and on *Madame Bovary*. The men who can do that sort of thing, and do it well, are not common. And for all this overpowering interest in all the arts, Huneker kept a corner of his brain free for the more coldly intellectual interests. He was enough of an amateur theologian to quote Harnack, enough of a philosopher to tilt with Bergson and William James. The chief interest of his last trip to Holland was a visit to De Vries, with whom he inspected primroses, and from whom he picked up enough of the theory of mutation to affect profoundly his thinking.

IV

All this no doubt seems far enough out of the way in a discussion of a literary critic. But as a matter of fact, it is strictly apropos. Huneker's mind was not of the sort that is divided into air-tight compartments, each containing its little isolated group of facts. He was the practitioner of a unique sort of comparative criticism. He compared, not only different literatures, but different arts. As a matter of pure theory, he denied the validity of this process, asserting that

> The respective substance of each art is different, and not even the extraordinary genius of Richard Wagner could fuse disparate dissimilarities.

And then, after making this polite bow to Professor Babbitt, he proceeded, with consistent inconsistency, to write of one art in terms of all the others. This is a dangerous process; in the hands of a tyro, a disastrous process. But Huneker makes of it something valuable. The particular function of the comparative critic is to bring together things far removed in time and space, and by a fortunate conjunction, to shed light on the things compared. Notable among such conjunctions is Huneker's parallel of Poe and Chopin—a parallel that would have occurred, I think, to no other critic, and one that sheds more light on Poe than half the volumes lately published about him. A characteristic and felicitous use of the terms of one art to illuminate a discussion of another is found in this sentence on Flaubert.

> His landscapes in the Dutch, tight, miniature style, or the large, luminous, loose manner of Holbein, or again full of the silver repose of Claude and the dark romantic beauty of Rousseau, are ravishing.

This airy leaping from literature to literature and from art to art sounds like the antics of a dilletante. But Huneker was no skimmer of surfaces. From pedantry, indeed, he was as far removed as from Puritanism. But underneath the brilliant surfaces of his essays lies a foundation of sound and thorough scholarship. There is no parading of authorities, no assumption of the ponderous manner of the academic critic. But the scholarship is there, nevertheless. The Ibsen study illustrates this point excellently. Not only had Huneker read every play of Ibsen's, including such little known works as *Catalina, Norma,* and *St. John's Night.* He had at his finger-tips the facts of Ibsen's life.

He was versed in dates of production. He had apparently read all the Ibsen critics worth reading—Brandes, Jaeger, Faguet, Archer, Wicksteed, and a dozen more. Even more solidly based is the volume on Chopin, with its evidence of original investigation, with its quotations from new sources, most of all with its laborious comparison of musical editings—the nearest approach to pedantry of anything in Huneker. Not only was Huneker, when the subject called for it, definitely scholarly in method. He had as wide a background of reading as the vast majority of professional scholars. One often hears the reproach leveled at journalistic critics that, while versed in modern literature, their knowledge stops at the year 1800. From such reproach Huneker is free. His reading can only be described as immense. Within the pages of *Steeplejack*—not a critical book, but an autobiography—one finds references to almost every classic author of importance. Here is a list gathered at random from a compass of about fifty pages—Cellini, Bossuet, Rabelais, Montaigne, Goethe, Aquinas, Dante, Cervantes, Bunyan, Horace. No American critic we have considered had read so widely, and few had read so well.

In spite of his keen intellect, in spite of his great

interest in ideas, Huneker had little trace, I think, of the specifically philosophical type of mind—the type of mind that seeks to organize its ideas into a system, to base its judgments on general principles which, put together, make a more or less complete philosophy of literature. Unlike his French masters, unlike most of the American critics who had preceded him, Huneker was not given to discussions of literature and criticism in the abstract. Except for one chapter in *Steeplejack,* headed "Criticism," Huneker's pronouncements on literary theory were limited to very incidental remarks dropped in the course of his examinations of specific writers. In theory, he recognizes the need of general principles of literary art. "The critic," he asserted, "should be an artist as to temperament, and he should have a credo." But as to the specific articles of this credo, Huneker was vague. Again we find him maintaining that "there must be standards, but the two greatest are sympathy and its half-brother sincerity." Sincerity may be a standard, but sympathy is obviously an attitude in the critic, and to call it a standard is to give oneself away rather badly. It is interesting to note that while Huneker was making these remarks, he plainly had in mind two of the neo-classic critics of his own time, W. C. Brownell and Irving Babbitt, of whom he speaks in admiring terms.

But having made these gestures in the direction of critical classicism, Huneker faced about, and asserted with far more force and clearness the utter subjectivity of criticism.

> No critic has ever settled anything.
>
> Neither praise nor blame should be the goal of the critic. To spill his own soul, that should be his aim.
>
> It is his prejudices that make vital a critic's work.
>
> Humbly to follow and register his emotions aroused by a masterpiece is his function. A little humility in a critic is a wise attitude.

These assertions are plainly pure impressionism, and in almost every instance, impressionism was Huneker's method. I think we may safely attribute his occasional classical pronouncements as mere illustrations of his intellectual sympathy with convincingly stated ideas.

Two more generalizations remain to be noted, and our examinations of Huneker's light baggage of critical doctrine will be done. Interested though he always was in ideas, moral ideas included, for moralistic criticism he had not the slightest use. In his reaction—a perfectly sound reaction—against the moralizing tone that has always marked a large section of American criticism, he ran to the other extreme. "Good art," he declared, "is never obscene; the only obscene art is bad art." Particularly disgustful to Huneker was the common trick of examining the life of a writer for offences against the current notion of morality, and transferring this condemnation to his literary work. Technique, in his view, was the morality of art, and with technique criticism should most busy itself. He even, following Henry James, the one previous American critic who seems to have influenced him in any respect, objects to criticism of subject. He impatiently exclaimed, "This harping on the theme of a drama—whether pleasant or unpleasant, dull, brilliant, or truthful—is eminently amateurish." He praised the criticism of Baudelaire because "he judged more of form than theme." In this respect, Huneker approached closely the critical attitude of Poe and of Stedman. But to follow it on all occasions is to place unnecessary and belittling restrictions on criticism, and Huneker, while preeminently a critic of form, paid no attention to this limitation when it got in his way. Like the greatest critics of all times, Huneker made his doctrines to suit the occasion, and he never balked at an inconsistency. His assertion, "I don't believe in movements or schematologies, or any one method of seeing and writing," applies perfectly to his own criticism. To shift one's position in this manner exposes one to all sorts of charges from the logically minded; it is, however, another of the marks of the great critic.

V

With Huneker, as with most critics, the theory is of far less importance than the method. Huneker's method was formed by lessons from many masters. An intense individualist, he was always interested in the personality of the writer. "Psychologue" was one of his pet words; and following in the steps of Sainte-Beuve, he played the psychologue to the writers he considered. And the writers who interested him most were the writers of striking and bizarre personality. Strindberg, Neitzsche, Wedekind, Dostoieffsky, Maupassant—these are among the most brilliant of his soul-portraits. "What," he exclaimed, "is more fascinating than a peep in the laboratory of a great artist's mind?" This interest in personality sometimes extends—as in the essay on Villiers de L'Isle Adam—to writers whose actual literary output Huneker valued not at all. The very titles of his volumes reveal this individualistic tendency. *Egoists, Iconoclasts, Bedouins, Unicorns*—the names speak for themselves.

To offset this interest in personality, which is an extreme form of Romanticism, Huneker, like a certain type of classicist, largely busied himself with questions of form and style. Like a true descendant of the great French critics, he was a stylist and a critic of style at all times. His repeated statement, "My most enduring artistic passions are for the music of Chopin and the prose of Flaubert," reveals the extent and the nature of his stylistic bent. He demanded that art should be artistic, consciously artistic. Thus we find him attacking Zola, not, like most critics of the day, for his moral ugliness, but because of his lack of finish. Eventually, this liking for the classically finished led Huneker to turn away from Whitman, one of his great early loves. But in general, Huneker's taste in style was catholic and catholicizing. Thus we find him admiring writers so far removed from him in temperament as Howells and Edith Wharton—largely because each is the master of a high prose style. He tasted with pleasure authors as far apart as Shaw and Pater, Newman and Anatole France.

Still more was Huneker concerned with form in

its larger aspects—and here he became genuinely classical. It is in his dramatic criticism that this element stands out most prominently. It even leads him to say a good word for Scribe. "Scribe is a wonderful technician. From him you may learn the playwright's trade." Huneker always discussed plays from the point of view of actual stage production, passing frequently into reminiscences of performances he had witnessed—in Paris, London, Berlin, Vienna, New York. His finest work in this direction is the long article on Ibsen, in the course of which he analyzes every play of Ibsen's, so accurately and searchingly that college professors use the essay as a text for the study of Ibsen's technique. It is a revealing side-light, both on Huneker and on the practice of technical criticism in general, that Huneker's condemnations of authors are always based on technical grounds. Thus, he first finds flaws in the novels of Stendhal and the plays of Shaw. But such technical condemnations occupy a comparatively small part of Huneker's criticism.

In this technical attitude toward literature, and this technical method of criticism, Huneker was in agreement with Poe, with Stedman, with James. But unlike these men, he did not stop at technique. We have noted his interest in the writer as a person; we have noted his interest in style, in the larger aspects of form. He was equally interested in ideas, and was always careful to lay bare, usually without accepting or rejecting, the ideas of his authors. As a result of this breadth of interest, he avoided the unsatisfying narrowness of which one is often conscious when reading critics who stop at form or who deal only with ideas. One gets from Huneker a more complete and rounded picture of the author under consideration than from almost any other critic of literature.

VI

But perhaps, after all, the chief quality of the great critic is his ability to write. Huneker could write. He had the journalist's trick of turning out clean copy. It is strange to find a man whose most lasting literary passion was for the prose of Flaubert saying, with entire truthfulness, "I never rewrite my books." His stylistic excellence was not the result of long and painful labor with the file; his brilliance was the natural and rapid utterance of a brilliant mind. He enjoyed doing tricks with words; he thought in clever sentences. He wrote in sentences; sometimes in sentences only. With characteristic self-awareness, he called *Steeplejack* "a book of beautiful quotations." Here is an extreme instance from the same volume.

> Envy is only a form of inverted admiration. Joseph Conrad speaks of pity as a special form of contempt. Stupidity is the great humorist, says George Moore. We live too much on the surface of our being. A philosopher has said that we live forward and think backward. Sorrow is the antiseptic of sick souls. Woman, declared the Fathers of the Church (shrewd psychologists), is the most potent engine of dolour that God has given Man. The French Revolution only destroyed ruins; the social edifice had been tottering for a century. . . . Intimate friends are, as a rule, disasters. Mythomania is a malady that spares few. Its real name is religion. Walt Whitman may have been a yellow dog, but he had a golden bark. Truth is always original. But what is truth? . . . I pause for breath.

This is parody, of course; but it is almost perfect parody, and parody itself is a highly intelligent sort of criticism.

Although Huneker's manner was always staccato, in his critical works this manner was under thorough control. Disjointed though his paragraphs may appear at first reading, this effect is often an optical illusion, the result of a dazzlement produced by the too continuous sparkle and glitter of his sentences. But beneath this coating of jewels there is a rigid steel structure. Every essay has its definite mark, toward which it flies straight as an arrow.

And after all, this staccato touch lent itself excellently to the expression of Huneker's fundamental impressionism, for Huneker was at bottom an impressionist. Huneker shared with Lowell—also an impressionist at heart—the great critical gift of catching and recording the peculiar excellence of an author in pointed and memorable phrase. The thing that interested Huneker in an author was not his measuring up to or deviation from any set standard, but the author's unique quality—the thing in which he differs from all other authors. To express that uniqueness was Huneker's main critical aim. Sometimes the trick was done in a phrase. Anatole France is "a consummate flowering of the dilletante." *Les Miserables* he beautifully described as a "windy apotheosis of vapid humanitarianism." Damning, but true, was the label he applied to Massenet and his like, "the puff-paste decorative school." He neatly hit off Franz Liszt, "who composed cadenzas with orchestral accompaniment and called them concertos." Here are more lengthy specimens.

The elemental things are his (Conrad's) chief concern, not the doings of dolls. He is not a propagandist. He never tries to prove anything.

Gorky transfers to his pages the odor of a starving, sweating humanity, its drunkenness, its explosions of rage, guttural cries of joy, and its all too terrible animalism. . . . Gorky, for all his moral nihilism, is as superstitious as a moujik. He shakes his fist at the eternal stars, and then makes the sign of the cross.

A latter-day pagan, with touches of the perverse, the grotesque, and the poetic; that seems to me Frank Wedekind.

Zola is a myopic romanticist, writing in a style both violent and tumified the history of his soul in the latrines of life.

There is a danger in being able to write like that, but Huneker never committed the crime of letting the sound carry away the sense. And for all his love for sparkle and glitter, Huneker could and did write pages of as solid and sensible exposition as any man of the Eighteenth Century.

VII

Insatiable in curiosity, cosmopolitan in training, writing in a style to stimulate the interest of the most jaded reader, filled with a highly communicable enthusiasm, Huneker made an incomparable literary pioneer. He has been reproached for his coldness toward American writers. Writing from an international viewpoint, he naturally had little use for those American writers who loomed large in our eyes during the last century only because of our literary isolation. But both the American writers whom he mentions and those of whom he omits to speak are evidence of his power of selection, his ability to pick out the best. It is just for those American writers to whose reputations time has added that he shows due admiration. We have noted his early devotion to Poe. Emerson seems to have influenced him profoundly. He quoted Thoreau with appreciation. Whitman he liked at first, later partly outgrew, but eventually accepted. Of his connection with the critical work of Henry James we have spoken. And these are the American writers to whom European criticism has paid most attention. Furthermore, Huneker retained to the end an interest in American literature in the making. No better illustration of his catholicity can be found than his esteem for Howells, who was in so many ways the very antithesis of Huneker. And he noted with appreciation the appearance of such ultramoderns as Edgar Saltus and Carl Van Vechten.

Toward English writers his attitude was always that of a discoverer. Back in 1888—the early date is significant—he was directly responsible for the first appearance in this country of an article by Shaw. He fought for George Moore when Moore was critically anathema in America. He was one of the first American critics to see that Havelock Ellis was something more than a technical psychologist. He hailed the dawn of the Irish Renaissance. He saw merit in James Joyce.

But others might have discovered these men for us. Huneker's special contribution was to make us better acquainted with contemporary continental literature. *Iconoclasts,* which appeared in 1905, was the first piece of criticism in this country to give serious attention to the continental dramatists.[1] It was also the first book by a major American critic to consider the drama as a subject for criticism. His studies in French literature make up a good half of his critical volumes. From Germany he brought back Nietzsche, Hauptmann, Sudermann, Wedekind; from Austria, Schnitzler; from Russia not only the better known men—Tolstoy, Turgeniev, Dostoieffsky, but such unheard of writers in that day as Gorky and Artzibascheff.

[1] There is one exception to this statement—Brander Matthews's book on the French playwrights, which appeared in 1888.

Merely to list the names of the foreign authors worth knowing with whom he helped to make us acquainted would fill a page.

This is a critical virtue, but it runs close to a critical defect. Huneker liked the thrill of discovery. He had a penchant for the new, the different, the outré. And one feels at times, that like Charles Lamb before him, he liked an author better for not being soiled by the admiration of the crowd. Thus he has been reproached for not keeping his eye fixed on the best things in literature, for preferring a second rate novelty to a greater but better known author. There is some truth in this, but also some justification for the attitude. Huneker wrote at the end of a century of great critical activity. Lowell and Hazlitt and Arnold and dozens of lesser men had already written almost ad nauseam on Chaucer and Shakespeare and Dante; and I suspect Huneker felt that all had been said on the major classics. Thus he deliberately turned to the equally necessary task of widening the literary horizon. I doubt whether he would have bettered Lowell on Spenser, and I am sure Lowell could not have written half so well on Shaw and Conrad. It was part of Huneker's work to correct the tendency of the greater critics to forget that literature was a living thing, that classics were still being written.

Catholicity, catholicism—the words constantly spring to one's lips when one speaks of Huneker. Now catholicity means something more than mental or critical spinelessness. The critic who likes everything is good for nothing. And Huneker, great as was his faculty of appreciation, far apart as were many of the things he liked, was never indiscriminate. His roving spirit paid no attention to the scholastic name-fences that hem in the admirations of lesser men. Classic and romantic, moral and immoral, realist and naturalist, hedonist and puritan—all were one to him, provided the author had something to say and knew how to say it. He could understand all kinds of excellence, but excellence of some kind there must be to win his approval. For the second-rate, the cheaply sentimental, the unintelligent, the badly-written, he had no use. And even in the authors whom he most liked, he was keen to distinguish between the good and the less good. He smelled sentimentalism in Chopin, deplored the lack of healthy earthiness in "preacher George" Shaw—"Beefsteak, old Scotch ale, a pipe, and Montaigne, are what Shaw needs for one year"

—noted the over-symbolism of *The Wild Duck,* soundly castigated Tolstoy for his anti-artistic heresy. He might have written excellent destructive criticism, armed as he was with knowledge, analytic power, humor, and the gift of slashing phrase. But his geniality and his utter lack of the reformer's zeal led him rather to pass over in silence the authors whose crimes outweighed their virtues. What critical fault-finding he did was only for the purpose of separating the real excellence of an author from the weaknesses and errors that block our clear view of that excellence. And it is a tribute to his discrimination that unlike Poe, he never lavished praise on an author undeserving of critical attention.

At the opposite pole of criticism from those critics who like a writer as he approaches some preconceived standard in the critic's mind, Huneker looked at each writer who was worth considering at all, not for resemblances, but for differences. What he wanted in an author was that author's individuality. And like a good critic, he threw logical consistency to the winds, and shifted his point of view from author to author. The essays composing the volume *Iconoclasts* are perhaps the finest illustration in the whole field of criticism of this

Protean flexibility of spirit. With Ibsen, we find Huneker talking of individualistic philosophy and the technique of the drama. He turned to Strindberg, and it was Strindberg himself that interested him, the massive, neurotic, tortured soul. The essay on Henri Becque is a rather coldly analytic discussion of characters and themes; the study of Hauptmann warm and humanitarian in tone. Into Shaw he poured volley after volley of arrow-pointed sentences, employing Shaw's own tricks of paradox, verbal gymnastics, wit, surprise. The succeeding essay, on Gorky, is a complete antithesis. Sombre in tone, savoring curiously the profound pessimism of the Russian, it is a fugue on the opening theme, "De profundis ad te clamavi." He praised Sudermann for his technical virtuosity, d'Annunzio for his evocations of passion, Maeterlinck for his twilight mysticism. The very style changed, as Huneker endeavored to accommodate his spirit to that of the author reviewed. A more catholic volume, a volume manifesting appreciation of more varieties of literary excellence, a volume that comes nearer to the critical ideal of judging an author in the light of his own aims, purposes, personality, exists, I think, nowhere.

VIII

From the main currents of American criticism, Huneker stood rather aloof. Some connection he had, as we have noted, with the work of previous American critics. Something of his individualistic attitude was probably derived from Emerson. Much of his attitude toward technical criticism came directly from Henry James, but Huneker consistently avoided the Jamesian restrictions on the range of the critic. At times he veered slightly toward the new humanistic school, ultimately derived from Lowell, and represented in that day by Babbitt and Brownell, though in general his critical attitude was the very opposite of theirs. But the main critical movement of the earlier part of Huneker's critical life was in the direction of dogmatic realism, a movement that, reverting to the methods of the Eighteenth Century, attempted to fix the novel by laying down for it a strict set of literary laws, and by damning all novelists who declined to comply. From the aims and methods of this movement Huneker turned with complete aversion. Not that he was an anti-realist; it was merely that he refused to be bound by the rules of any school of literary art, realistic, naturalistic, veritistic, or what you will. With the rather heavily serious moral attitude of the realistic school Huneker was also in complete disagreement. He represented rather that general tendency toward the liberalizing of literary opinion, both in matters of form and in questions of morals, that we have noted as one of the leading tendencies in American criticism from 1815 on.

Owing to the very nature of his work, its vagueness in theory, its eclecticism of spirit, Huneker left no immediate critical descendants. Traces of his influence can indeed be found in many quarters. His interest in the drama was, I think, one of the many contributing factors in that renaissance of the American drama which began in the nineties and flowered only yesterday. His literary cosmopolitanism left its mark on nearly all succeeding American critics, most notably perhaps on Ernest Boyd, who seems at times a conscious imitator of Huneker. His impatience with moral attitudes in literary criticism has been adopted by the literary radicals of Mr. Mencken's school, men from whom he is in many respects far removed. But in general we may say that Huneker stands as a great critical monolith at the opening of the Twentieth Century.

To understand all schools and to belong to none; to appreciate the good in literature under a thousand varying forms; to experience constant and unwearied delight in reading, and to express that delight, that gusto, in contagious terms; to penetrate, with lightning keenness, the secret of an author's power; to reveal that secret in dazzling and unforgettable phrase—these are the achievements of a great critic. And above all these, to flash constantly upon the reader glimpses of a personality as rare, as fascinating, as that of any author whom he discusses, is to write criticism that is in itself literature. There are moods in which one is disposed to call Huneker the greatest of American critics. This is probably excessive. At any rate, he stands, with Lowell and Poe and James, in the very front rank of American criticism.

CRITICAL WORKS OF JAMES GIBBONS HUNEKER
ISSUED IN BOOK FORM

Mezzotints in Modern Music — Scribner, New York, 1899

Chopin: the Man and his Music — Scribner, New York, 1900

Overtones, a Book of Temperaments — Scribner, New York, 1904

Iconoclasts, a Book of Dramatists — Scribner, New York, 1905

Egoists, a Book of Supermen — Scribner, New York, 1909
Promenades of an Impressionist — Scribner, New York, 1910
Franz Liszt — Scribner, New York, 1911
The Pathos of Distance — Scribner, New York, 1913
Ivory Apes and Peacocks — Scribner, New York, 1915
Unicorns — Scribner, New York, 1917
Steeplejack — Scribner, New York, 1920
Bedouins — Scribner, New York, 1920
Variations — Scribner, New York, 1921
Letters of James Gibbons Huneker — Scribner, New York, 1922

I have included here volumes on music and painting, since it seems to me that without them one cannot begin to understand Huneker.

CHAPTER IX

SHERMAN

I

THE end of the Nineteenth Century left American criticism in a fairly settled condition. The last New England writer of the great tradition had passed from the stage; the respective niches the writers of that tradition were to occupy in the Hall of Fame had been settled. As far as American poetry was concerned, opinion had progressed hardly at all from the orthodoxy established by Stedman in 1880. Barrett Wendell's *Literary History of America*, published in 1900, seemed to state with absolute finality the creed of all future historians of American literature when dealing with the Nineteenth Century. In the field of the novel, realism was the accepted doctrine; and Howells was its great exemplar. Signs of revolt might have been discerned in Huneker, but he, although widely read, was somewhat without the pale.

And then, in the second decade of the Twentieth

Century, something happened. The publication, in 1913, of John Macy's *Spirit of American Literature,* marks the outbreak of the last great revolution in American literary thought. In this daring volume Macy, setting aside the generally accepted verdicts on the classical American writers, went back to the originals, and examined the whole case afresh. His conclusions were startling indeed. Echoing Emerson's judgment of seventy years before, he decided that the vast mass of American writing, especially of American poetry, was feeble, second-rate, derivative. From his re-examination, the figures of Poe, Thoreau, Twain, Whitman emerged as the really great among American writers. The New England poets, on the other hand, Longfellow, Lowell, Whittier, were given very short shrift. And Howells, the dean of American letters, was treated with an irreverence positively shocking.

This was bad enough, but this was only the beginning. Macy was soon exceeded by critics far more radical. Van Wyck Brooks, Randolph Bourne, Carl Van Doren, George Jean Nathan, each contributed his bit to the revolt. But the full flowering of radicalism was reached in the work of H. L. Mencken, who developed from a purely literary critic into a sort of universal iconoclast, attacking current orthodoxies in religion, in politics, in morals, as well as in literature. Mencken's chief work was, perhaps, in the direction of purely destructive criticism, the only following in American criticism of the early and generally forgotten practice of Poe. Coincident with this critical movement ran the development of the satiric novel, best exemplified in Sinclair Lewis, and a corresponding vein of satiric poetry initiated by the *Spoon River Anthology* of Edgar Lee Masters. And all this literary stir was but one side of the general tendency of American thought during this period toward iconoclastic radicalism in everything.

Like all violent movements, this radical criticism provoked a corresponding reaction. More, Babbitt, Brownell—older men these—raised in opposition the standard of the "New Humanism," a body of critical doctrine which went back for its origins to the anti-romantic and neo-classic principles of Lowell. Between the fighters in these opposing armies war was merrily waged, raising American criticism from the somnolent state into which it had fallen in the gentlemanly hands of Messrs. Stedman, Mabie, and Woodberry, and converting it into the bloodiest of literary battlefields. Now nothing catches the public eye like a good fight;

and for a decade, from 1915 to 1925, criticism became perhaps the leading form of literary activity in America. For the first time in the history of American literature a critic—Mencken—was the best known and the most influential of American writers. At first the radicals seemed to have much the best of the duel, but the balance was somewhat restored by the appearance of a new figure on the humanistic side—Stuart P. Sherman.

II

Born in Iowa in 1881, Sherman took Horace Greeley's advice in reverse; as a young man, he went East, first to Williams and then to Harvard, where he received his doctor's degree in 1906. During the next decade, as teacher at Northwestern and Illinois, as editor of school and college texts, as contributor to *The Nation,* as co-editor of the *Cambridge History of American Literature,* he was beginning to build up a reputation as a scholar-critic who actually had something to say and could say it with considerable force and point.

The appearance, in 1917, of his first volume, *Matthew Arnold: How to Know Him,* summed up, in a sense, this period of preparation. More important, for our purposes, it pointed the way clearly to the future. In this volume, which is, incidentally, the best study of Arnold that has been written, Sherman revealed himself as an enthusiastic Arnoldian. He approved Arnold's reverence for the classics, his severe discrimination, his passion for controversy, his missionary zeal, even his excursions into the outlandish realms of theology and morals and political theory—excursions so bitterly bewailed by that purest of belle-lettrists, George Saintsbury. Even if one is inclined to think Saintsbury the nearer right in this matter, there can be no question that Sherman is the better Arnoldian.

It was as a devout follower, then, of the sublime and superior Matthew that Sherman set out to study his contemporaries. Now Arnold was above all things a crusader, waging relentless war against British Philistinism. Sherman likewise, in his next volume, *On Contemporary Literature,* published also in 1917, went forth to war. His particular opponent, in this battle of the books, was Naturalism, which he defined as "a representation of life based on a theory of animal behavior." Arnoldian in his clarity and emphasis, Sherman left no doubt in anyone's mind as to just what he was driving at. The title page of the book bears, as a text for the whole volume, this quotation from Arnold: "Man must begin, know this, where nature ends." Sherman later repeated and amplified the text in this form:

> The great revolutionary task of the nineteenth-century thinkers was to put man into nature. The great task of twentieth-century thinkers is to get him out again.

From the vantage point of this critical platform, Sherman surveyed contemporary literature, judging and condemning authors as they fall short of fulfilling the aim here indicated as their proper one.

The great exponent of naturalism in modern literature Sherman found to be Dreiser; Dreiser, therefore, was Sherman's particular aversion, in whom he could see no literary excellence whatever. He is "the vulgarest voice yet heard in American literature." He "colors the news." His method is the "certification of the unreal by the irrelevant." Less culpable than Dreiser, but addicted to Naturalism, and therefore literary sinners, Sherman found most of the outstanding figures of modern literature. Wells is a "Utopian Naturalist," the advocate of pseudo-science, seeking to make "whim and the will of Wells prevail." Moore is an "Aesthetic Naturalist," a "pretty writer," whose realistic novels are worthless because inconsistent with the rest of his literary output, and therefore insincere. Synge is an "Exotic," viewing man only as a spectacle to be enjoyed. All are essentially bad.

While the critical doctrine which Sherman is here expounding is less reminiscent of Arnold than of Professor Babbitt of Harvard, the critical method is the method of Arnold. Like Arnold, Sherman is judicial. He definitely places every author whom he handles; the sheep are clearly separated from the goats. Again like Arnold, Sherman finds most of his contemporaries wanting. Like Arnold, he demands high seriousness and the expression of moral ideas in his authors. Thus Meredith, of all the authors considered in the volume, receives fullest praise, not because he is a great literary artist, but because he is a great spiritual leader. Many even of Arnold's minor traits reappear in Sherman; his snobbishness, which regards Mark Twain with disapproval on account of his vulgarity; his trick of hammering on a theme until not even the stupidest reader in a stupid public can miss the point; even his curious antipathy to Shelley.

Some of these Arnoldian borrowings are clearly defects. But along with them Sherman learned from Arnold two lessons of the highest importance to a critic. He learned to perfection the art of critical exposition; he was the most masterly reporter of literature of his time. Whether he approved or condemned, he never left an author without giving the reader an unmistakably clear notion of what the author was like. I heartily disagree with Sherman's judgment of Wells; yet I take away from his essay a picture clearer and sharper in outline, a picture far more representative of Wells, than from half a dozen gushing tributes of praise by enthusiastic disciples of that omniscient seer. Closely allied with this indebtedness to Arnold was a second, of perhaps greater importance. Arnold's greatest critical virtue lies in his ability to get at the heart of an author—to point out and lay aside all the minor qualities and characteristics with which the spirit of a writer is often mistakenly identified, and coming at last to the central core, to place his finger on the essential thing, and say, "This is the man." This, the best of the Arnoldian elements in Sherman, can be seen most clearly in his study of Henry James. Here Sherman was bothered by no disturbing questions of naturalism and humanism; his mind was free to work untroubled by the moralistic bias; and the result was the finest study of James that has been written. Most studies of James lose themselves in discussions of his style, or his realism, or his so-called international viewpoint. All these Sherman examined, but only as veils to be drawn aside, until at last we stand before the man himself, who in spite of all his talk about "provincialism" and "saturation," is at heart an idealist, an "aesthetic idealist," whose whole artistic life was one prolonged and incessant quest for beauty. This is the insight of a great critic.

In spite, however, of all these borrowings from Arnold, Sherman was too much of a positive personality to be a mere copyist. Agreeing with Arnold in so many points, he nevertheless diverged sharply from his master in one respect of the highest importance. Unlike Arnold, who preserved the Anglican contempt for Puritanism long after he had lost all trace of Anglican dogma, Sherman was a Puritan and an advocate of Puritanism. With Puritanic distrust of a mere literature that does not further the cause of morality, he condemned Mark Twain because he "does not give us much help toward realizing our best selves." He praised Bennett for asserting that "the great principles, spiritual and moral, remain intact." Most characteristically Puritan of all was his glorification of the "impulse to refrain."

For all its obvious faults, *On Contemporary Lit-*

erature is a fighting book, therefore an exhilarating book. Discerning clearly the two main streams of literary criticism in his day, Sherman definitely ranked himself with the neo-classicists—Shorey, More, Brownell, and Babbitt. More than that, he here revealed himself the ablest warrior of the company. Far more alive to contemporary currents than More, more active and more productive than Brownell, he was also far more sane and sensible than the erratic and lop-sided anti-Romanticist, Professor Babbitt, from whom, however, he had obviously learned much.

III

Between the publication of this volume, and that of its successor, *Americans*, in 1922, many things happened. For one, there was a war. In Sherman, no cloistered recluse, but a man very much alive and very much aware of the world about him, the events of 1914–18 produced a mental revolution. One of Sherman's most engaging traits appears in his habit of starting off each of his volumes with a preface, in which he warns the reader, with the utmost candor, of his exact purpose in that particular volume. The preface to *Americans* thus tells us just what the war had done to Sherman. It found him an Arnoldian; it left him something perilously near to a Rotarian. In the volumes of 1917, he had been a cosmopolitan, a literary catholic, deriving most of his doctrines from the great central cultural tradition of Europe. He was now a nationalist, an American, almost a hundred per cent American. With war-heightened patriotism, which included of necessity a hatred of all things Teutonic, he announced his intention of revealing his vision of "the spirit of America as the clear-eyed among our poets and statesmen have seen her." His purpose was "to encourage readers to keep open the channel of their national traditions and to scrutinize contemporary literature in the light of their national past." With this object in view, he selected ten eminent Americans, and attempted to trace through them the presence or the absence of this great American tradition. This tradition, as a reader of the preceding volumes might have guessed, he identified with Puritanism.

In this intense interest in Americanism in literature, Sherman was but moving with his time. One mark that distinguished all the American critics of the day, whether radical or conservative, from their predecessors, was their almost exclusive attention to American literature. To such older critics as Lowell,

James, and Huneker, American literature had been at best a very minor interest. Even Poe, Stedman, and Howells were fully as much occupied with English and foreign books as with American. But from 1913 on, American literature and the revision of the literary history of America were the great battlegrounds of criticism, and to balance *The Ordeal of Mark Twain* and *The Opinions of a Literary Radical* we have *Americans* and *Standards.*

But before he proceeded to his constructive labors in tracing this great American tradition, Sherman had a word to say to the opponents of the received American tradition in literature—to the radical critics of the younger generation. He was ready now to cross swords with Mr. Mencken. In the first essay of the book, a piece of writing as lively as any flowing from the pen of his adversary, Sherman delivered the first blow in that six-year duel which was the most stirring spectacle perhaps in modern American letters. Thus he pictures Mr. Mencken arriving on the literary scene.

> He leaps from the saddle with sabre flashing, stables his horse in the church, shoots the priest, hangs the professors, and exiles the academy, burns the library and the university, and, amid the smoking ashes, erects a new school of criticism on modern German principles, which

he traces through Spingarn to Goethe, but which I should be inclined to trace rather to Eckermann.

But Sherman could wield other weapons than the Menckenian bludgeon. From Arnold he had learned the exasperating trick of getting on higher ground than his adversary, and talking down to him. With a mixture of slyness and superiority worthy of Arnold himself, Sherman ends the essay by quoting with deceptive calmness a little maxim from Joubert, that is absolutely devastating when applied to Mencken: "Ou il n'y a point de delicatesse, il n'y a point de litterature."

It is not necessary to follow in detail Sherman's heroic endeavor to trace the great American and Puritan tradition through the works of Franklin and Emerson and Hawthorne and Whitman. As individual portraits these essays are excellent, particularly that on Whitman, which reveals in Sherman a breadth of sympathy rather lacking in his previous volume. But as pieces of evidence in Sherman's case for Puritanism, they have the common and rather grave fault of proving the opposite of what they are meant to prove. The real strength of these men—and Sherman's exposition should make the fact clear to the dullest reader—is not that they are representative Puritans, but rather that they were all in some degree in revolt against Puritanism. They were the radicals, the revolutionaries, the moderns—in other words, the Menckens.

IV

It is one of the platitudes of literary history that there comes a time in the growth of nearly every critic when he tires of being merely a critic, and aspires to the reputation of a prophet. Thus Arnold, in mid-career, turned educational philosopher, biblical critic, and advocate of religious liberalism. Thus Lowell emerged into political thought with *Democracy and Other Addresses*. Thus even Poe, with whom literature was almost completely divorced from life, in his melancholy last days, his brain weakened by disease and disappointment and hunger, wrote *Eureka*. And thus, in these last days, we have seen Mr. Mencken turn politician, theologian, philosopher, moralist—all the while denying, with considerable asperity, that he was doing anything of the sort.

About 1920, Sherman was seized by the same fever. There had, of course, been symptoms of it in his work from the start, but in the companion volume to *Americans, The Genius of America*, published in 1923, the disease was first revealed in its acute stage. Here we have a curious instance of reaction. One of the leading tendencies of American criticism, from the founding of the *North American Review* to the last volume of James Huneker, had been the gradual separation of literature and morals—a separation faulty in theory, but exceedingly salutary in its effects. Against this tendency, Sherman resolutely set his face. Believing that the art-for-art's-sake theory is responsible for the present low esteem in which the arts are held by the great majority of good Americans, believing that if the critic calls art play you cannot expect the business man to take art seriously, Sherman attempted to restore literature to its proper place as the teacher of sound ethics. Theoretically, there is much to be said for this view of literature, but it seems invariably to lead the critic who attempts to realize it in practice into fearful aberrations of judgment. Sherman was generally a good reasoner, but under the influence of this doctrine, he brought forth such strange pseudo-syllogisms as this:

> An artist is a man living in society. A great artist is a great man living in a great society. When a great artist expresses himself completely, it is found invariably that he has expressed, not merely himself, but also the dom-

inant thoughts and feelings of the men with whom he lives.

The second leading theme of *The Genius of America* was again the defence of Puritanism against Mr. Mencken and his Teutonic hordes. It was a gallant attempt, as are all defences of lost causes; so persuasive, indeed, is Sherman's dialectic that at first reading the defence seems almost convincing. But before we agree with the plausible Sherman that Puritanism is a novel and beautiful ideal, let us consider how he defines that much-muddied term.

> Puritanism is not a fixed form of life; it is a formative spirit, an urgent exploring and creative spirit. . . . The Puritan is an iconoclast, an image-breaker; and when he is convicted of self-idolatry, he is the first, beautiful and strong in wrath, to raise the hammer and shatter his own image.

The Puritan is not morally intolerant; he is perpetually dissatisfied with the past; he is the formative force in that elusive phenomenon, the modern spirit. His true representatives are Milton and Bunyan and Emerson. Now the trouble with this definition is that like Norris's definition of realism, it is making words mean what you want them to mean and not what the majority of mankind means by them. If this conception is correct, then Mencken is a Puritan. And so is Wells. And so are Sinclair Lewis, and Floyd Dell, and James Huneker, and all the radical army with whom Sherman was waging bitter war. Obviously, when Sherman crowns the Puritan with a halo of light, and when Mencken hits him with a brick, they are looking at different creatures—creatures, indeed, of different species. The Puritan whom Sherman praises is the historical Puritan, the originator of revolt; the Puritan whom Mencken attacks is his degenerate descendant, the product of revolt that has hardened into an orthodoxy itself. And the difference between these men is the difference between Martin Luther and William Jennings Bryan.

As *The Genius of America* plainly indicates, Sherman was far indeed from being the conventional cloistered scholar. He was a man of his time, exceptionally susceptible to the influence of his surroundings, and reflecting their pressure in his works. This is an excellent preservative against fossilization, but it has its dangers. The young man who had emerged from Harvard an Arnoldian and a devout classicist had become, in 1923, professor of English and dean of men at the University of Illinois, one of the largest of that saurian species, the western state university. In the process he had also become a patriot, a prohibitionist, and a democrat. And thus we find the former student of *Culture and Anarchy* defending "education by the people" as practised in the western universities against the snobbishness of privately endowed eastern institutions, and attacking such upholders of the older culture as Katherine Fullerton Gerould. This was a startling about-face. But there are still, in this his worst volume, echoes of better things from the past, and faint forecasts of better things to come. With charming inconsistency, in the essay called *Vocation*, an essay highly Emersonian in thought, and even aping Emerson's disconnected-sentence style, Sherman attacked the mid-western ideal of "Service" as embodied in the Y.M.C.A. and the "foreign field." He acknowledged the truth of the old Arnoldian criticism of American life as dull and ugly. And in the last essay of the volume, he turned once more to the aristocratic and Arnoldian conception of university education—education, not as a means of uplifting the masses, but as an engine for producing the governors of society. Wide enough in his sympathies to love both literature and life, Sherman saw that "every attempt to make an educated man without connecting him with the historical tradition is myopic and absurd; but, on the other hand, all the tradition that does not come to a focus in the present hour is out of focus; it is presbyopic and inefficient."

The high spot of Sherman's acquired midwestern Rotarianism was reached in the opening essay of his 1924 volume, *Points of View.* In this essay, which bore the title *Towards an American Type,* Sherman, disregarding the lifeless dogmas which bear the name of religion, set out in his perennial search for the true American religion as manifested in actual American life. America, he discovered, has a religion; and the gods of its worship are five. They are Cleanliness, Health, Swift Mobility, Publicity, and Athletics. So far, so good. These are the gods of America. The curious thing is that Sherman, for all his deep cultural background, instead of recognizing them as the tin idols they are, found them true and beautiful deities. What do these gods really mean? Cleanliness? Schools with tiled and nickel-plated lavatories, and a hundred dusty volumes in the library. Swift Mobility? The limousine at the curb and "Show that Fellow the Door" on the Victrola. Publicity? Billboards on the Palisades. Health? Dr. Almus Pickerbaugh and Senator

Copeland. Athletics? Ten-thousand-dollar-a-year coaches and two-thousand-dollar-a-year professors. It is hard to see how anyone could be deceived. But one must recognize this about Sherman. Keen-minded and open-eyed in the perception of facts, in their interpretation he was one of the most hopeless optimists on record. He was so determined to think well of America that he could give his admiration to these things; things which seem, to a critic less fortunate in hope, the very demons that beset us. Though facile optimism is an amiable weakness, it is a strange trait in an Arnoldian.

There were other blots on the volume—Sherman's curious attempt to prove that Samuel Butler was personally a cad and a blackguard; true enough, possibly, but of no weight whatever in a discussion of Butler as a writer.[1]

But these sins were more than atoned for by certain signs of change. Some of Sherman's major errors sprang, in fact, from the excess of one of his virtues—his openness and receptivity. For in spite of all his dogmas and prejudices, he was if anything

[1] The reader will note that here Sherman returned to the critical methods of the Peabodies and the Everetts. It is all very well to be interested in the personality of a writer, but to attempt to translate one's moral judgment of his personality into a literary judgment of his books has been one of the besetting sins of American criticism.

over-susceptible to the currents of life about him—a rare enough fault in a professor. And as this quality had led him into strange heresies, it was finally to bring him to the truth. No man with Sherman's mental alertness and breadth of taste could long survey the spectacle of modern American literature without finding there some qualities to admire. In this same volume, then, which contains Sherman's worst yielding to his uncouth environment, we find the first symptoms of his growing sympathy with the new forces in American literature. He began to profess admiration for the "Dreiser-Hecht school of monoptic novelists and for the Menckenian school of monoptic critics." He saw that the hate-sharpened satire of these men was the proper corrective for our customary rose-pink idealism. This admiration was, of course, hedged about with reservations. But his principal ground of quarrel with these authors—that they are not sufficiently in love with American life, and are therefore incapable of understanding it fully—was an objection by no means pointless.

It is always interesting and frequently productive of high comedy to apply a man's dogmas to his own acts. If complete understanding is born only of love, we can well apply to *On Contemporary Literature*

Sherman's own pet adjective, "monoptic." When that work was written, Sherman was very plainly not in love with the greater part of contemporary literature. And it is certainly true that as his liking for contemporary literature grew more and more genuine, so did his criticism of it gain in breadth and soundness. How sound was Sherman's taste, and how keen his insight, when that taste and insight were free to function, unclouded by perverting doctrines, is admirably demonstrated by the two essays which chiefly atone for the errors of *Points of View*—the studies of Disraeli and Sinclair Lewis.

The first of these studies illustrated well the ability, possessed by Sherman in common with most good critics, to get rid of a dogma when the dogma is in the way. In politics, all men are born Gladstonians or Disraelites; Sherman was a Gladstonian. But on examining the two men, in spite of his conviction that Gladstone's was the purer influence in politics, he succumbed to Dizzy's charm, and gave us a portrait of the author-statesman almost fit to be compared with Lytton Strachey's. The literary critic had at last overcome the Puritan moralist.

Better still is the study of Sinclair Lewis. That Lewis, who has made "Rotarian" a cuss-word, should be the first of modern American writers to win Sherman's full approval is at first sight astonishing. But the essay convinces one that Sherman's Rotarianism was merely a superficial and transitional phase of his growth, due to the pressure of environment. Sherman's sympathy with Lewis was the result of something far more fundamental. A closer inspection shows the two men to have much in common: both possessing alert intelligence and keen observation; both possessed by the critical spirit. Sherman's deep-rooted Arnoldism found satisfaction in the truth that Lewis's novels are all "a criticism of contemporary life with special reference to its interest and beauty." And Lewis, like Sherman, was Arnoldian in spirit, condemning in American life the very things—standardization, materialism, ugliness—that would assuredly have annoyed the urbane and superior Matthew. It is not difficult to see then, why Sherman concluded that Lewis "is conspiring with the spirit of the times to become the most interesting and important novelist in America." At the close of the essay, Sherman, fired with enthusiasm, broke into prophecy.

Eventually, if Mr. Lewis does not wish to pass for a hardened pessimist he will have to produce a hero qualified to register in some fashion the result of his own quest for the desirable; he will have to give us his Portrait of a

Lady, his Warrington and his Colonel Newcome. Meanwhile I am very well content to applaud the valor of his progress through Vanity Fair.

And, as if in answer, Mr. Lewis wrote *Arrowsmith*.

My Dear Cornelia (1924), that curious Irish stew of literary criticism, Platonic dialogue on morals, and moon-struck sentimental romance with melodramatic episodes thrown in to point the moral, added nothing to Sherman's reputation. But it is interesting to the student of his career, showing more fully than any other of his works one shining facet of his mind. In his work at the University of Illinois, Sherman was of necessity brought into close and frequent contact with that strange apparition, the younger generation. Now Sherman was the kind of man who could not be long in contact with any man, book, group, or institution without making a valiant attempt at understanding. He made heroic efforts to comprehend this so un-Arnoldian younger generation. The trait appeared earlier than this book; *The Genius of America* bears as its subtitle *Studies in Behalf of the Younger Generation.* His real charge against Mencken had been that Mencken was undermining the morals of the young folks. But in this volume he made his first avowed attempt to see what the younger generation was about, to understand it fully, and if possible to sympathize with its aims. Setting up Cornelia as the representative of the conservative viewpoint, the viewpoint of the shocked elders, he answered in person her attacks. After thus conducting a dialogue between the two halves of his mind, he arrived, with characteristic optimism, at the conclusion that the younger generation is after all sane and sound, and that if it will only learn to obey the Eighteenth Amendment, it will go to heaven along with its sainted ancestors.

V

With this book, the second phase of Sherman's career came to an end. In the spring of 1924, the management of the New York *Herald-Tribune* summoned Sherman from Illinois to take the editorship of that journal's rather insignificant book review. This act produced two important results. It raised the *Tribune's* review, now renamed *Books*, from its lowly position to that of the ablest and liveliest weekly book review in the country. What is more to our purpose, it accelerated mightily those changes in Sherman which we have seen incipient in his previous work. Removed from an academic environment to the swirl and bustle of New York, brought into intimate contact with literature in the making, no man as thoroughly alive as Sherman could have remained unchanged. Fully aware of this change in himself, he set it forth with engaging frankness in the preface to his next and last volume, *Critical Woodcuts*. In this preface, only four pages in length, there is summed up a whole literary confession of faith.

I have never taken a vow to carry any opinion unaltered to the grave: and if it can be proved tonight that I have learned absolutely nothing since morning, I shall be dismayed.

The first duty of a commentator on current literature, as it appears to me, is to present a fairly full and veracious report of what is going on.

The critic is a scout seeking for the main channel of intellectual and emotional activity in his own tract of time, recurring constantly to the point where the full rush of living waters comes in from the past, and eagerly searching for the point where the flood breaks out of the backwater and through the dams, and streams away into the future.

All human activities have, up their sleeves, an ulterior object and ultimate justification in happier living: and it is rather specially the "function" of critics to be engaged in an incessant, untiring exploration in quest of "the good life."

Patient search usually discovers some refreshing virtue wherever there has been exhibited any unusual display of energy.

From these five statements only, one might easily deduce all of Sherman's best qualities. One sees in the first his openness and receptivity; in the second, his masterly ability as a literary expositor; in the third, his interest in ideas and his literary descent from Arnold; in his fourth, his profound concern for morals; and in the fifth, his undaunted resolution to find good in everything.

In form, *Critical Woodcuts* differed widely from Sherman's earlier books. The papers composing it were written as leading articles for *Books;* they are therefore much shorter than the studies in the previous volumes, averaging as they do about three thousand words apiece. They differ widely in method also. All of Sherman's earlier criticism had been distinctly judicial. The authors under review were definitely placed, both with regard to contemporary literary, and in comparison with the great figures of the past. In these shorter studies, on the other hand, the attempt is rather to tell the reader what the author is like, to pick out his salient qualities, and to leave the verdict to the future, though there is, of necessity, a certain amount of implied approval or condemnation lying behind the mere exposition. But far more important than these surface changes is the great inner change that the volume reveals.

The book is full of about-faces. In 1916, Sherman had unsparingly condemned Wells. In 1925 we find him addressing Wells in the following apostrophe:

> You are no realist, Mr. Wells. But you have been a brave myth-maker and a heartening poet to the Intellectuals of your time. You have turned an entire generation of novelists and readers from contemplating the fatal forces of heredity and environment and instinct to considering the godlike power of an intelligent will to control instinct, heredity and environment.

Wells, then, is a Humanist, after all. Wells, is, however, a gentleman of fairly well-established reputation. To discover excellence in him is no great feat. It is more surprising to find Sherman lauding Sherwood Anderson as "the impassioned interpreter of day-dreams of common people." It is still more astounding to find him defending D. H. Lawrence against the attacks of Doctor Collins. In 1916, Sherman had rashly asserted: "If anything is dead, the aesthetic movement that took shape in the seventies is dead." But in 1925, considering the worst of the bad boys of that movement, Sherman decides that "Oscar Wilde's works are in English literature and they are likely to remain there."

But there was always one adversary who could be depended upon to induce Sherman to seize his Damascus blade and sally forth to battle. And that he could wield his weapon with no diminishing of his former skill and vigor is proved by the essay entitled *H. L. Mencken as Liberator*. His first blow landed on Mencken's most sensitive spot—his carefully concealed, Heine-like vein of poetry. But over this hidden poet, Sherman explains, lies a blond Nordic—"a hard fighter, a hard eater, a hard drinker, a hard boaster, reverencing women but keeping them in the kitchen—a man, in short, with no sentiment or nonsense about him." Another of Mencken's little failings, according to Sherman, is his lack of reverence for the truth, as evidenced by his perversions of literary history. Hard hits, all of these, but worse was in store.

I have sworn to myself not to end this review on the note of detraction, but to bring it back to the note of sincere admiration on which it started. Though Mencken lacks the patience, the discrimination, and the "organ for truth" which the critic of a civilized minority ought to possess, he has other great talents. He is, as I have said elsewhere, alive. He has been the occasion of life in others. He has the rare gift of stirring people up and making them strike an attitude, and at least start on the long process of becoming intelligent beings.[2] And he is be-

[2] It is perhaps a bit dangerous, in a work of this sort, to venture an opinion on so controversial a subject as Mr. Mencken. But it seems to me that Sherman has here hit at the root of the Menckenian matter by pointing out that Mencken is to be considered, not as a great critic, but as a great educator.

ginning to quote from good authors, He is beginning to quote shyly from the New Testament in the Latin of the Vulgate. What may that bode? No one who has followed his work as carefully and hopefully as I have these many years can have failed to recognize that his obvious calling is to some form of ministry. From the first he has exhibited the desk-beating proclivities, the over-strained voice, the tumid phrases which one associates with the popular orator. Years ago I pointed out the absurdity of his presenting himself chiefly as an aesthetic interpreter when every drop of his blood seethes with moral passion and every beat of his heart summons him to moral propaganda.

Thus neatly he denied to Mr. Mencken every quality which that gentleman has publicly claimed, and attributed to him just those virtues the attribution of which was most likely to cause him to emit loud roars of rage. This was not only clever; it was largely true. But it was the fighter's last blow. In the summer of 1926, the literary world was shocked by the news of Sherman's death by drowning.

VI

We are still a little too close to Sherman in point of time, we are far too deeply engaged in the critical war in which he fought, to determine with any finality his place in American literature. But since the canon of his work is unfortunately closed, certain conclusions in regard to it may perhaps be drawn safely. In his earlier work he was, as we have seen, the leading exponent of that neo-classic or humanistic movement, which leads back, through the work of More and Brownell and Woodberry, to its American source in Lowell's writings of the middle period of his life. One may or may not agree with the doctrines of this movement; but they are, at least as stated by Sherman, intelligent doctrines, and I think rather salutary doctrines in the present state of American letters.

In his later work, Sherman was apparently drawing away very rapidly from the viewpoint of dogmatic humanism. In this there was both loss and gain. Sherman's later work is vastly more sympathetic, more tolerant, more catholic, than his earlier. But tolerance, breadth of mind, is apt to mean a certain dulling of the fighting edge. Thus one misses, in this last volume, the reasoned viewpoint, the philosophical backbone, the controversial sharpness of the earlier books.[3] The moderns have lately

[3] Huneker and Sherman began their work at opposite poles: Huneker was a journalist, a Roman Catholic, and a pupil of Sainte-Beuve and the French critics; Sherman a trained and professional scholar, a Puritan, and a follower of Arnold. Yet, in this last volume, Sherman was writing in the spirit, and almost in the method of Huneker, except that he still retained something of the controversial element, almost lacking in Huneker.

had it rather too much their own way in criticism, and I for one have been delighted to see the banner of conservatism upborne by so valiant and skilful a warrior as Sherman.

CRITICAL WRITINGS OF STUART P. SHERMAN

Matthew Arnold: How to Know Him	Bobbs Merrill, Indianapolis, 1917
On Contemporary Literature	Henry Holt, New York, 1917
Americans	Scribner, New York, 1922
The Genius of America	Scribner, New York, 1923
My Dear Cornelia	Atlantic Monthly Press, Boston, 1924
Points of View	Scribner, New York, 1924
Critical Woodcuts	Scribner, New York, 1926
The Main Stream	Scribner, New York, 1927
Life and Letters of Stuart P. Sherman	Zeitlin and Woodbridge, New York, 1929

Epilogue

The death of Sherman brings our survey to an appropriate close. We have here examined a little over a century of literary criticism in America, attempting to study in some detail the work of the more important critics, and to trace the general currents of critical thought and literary taste which flow through the period. In the course of this study we have noted four great revolutions in criticism. The year 1815, which we have selected as marking the beginning of real literary criticism in this country, found the Eighteenth Century still in full sway. The Romantic revolution came late in America. Begun by Dana in the twenties, carried on by Longfellow, it was finally consummated by Lowell and Poe in the forties. In the seventies comes the Aesthetic revolution led by Stedman, itself a development of the early romanticism of Lowell and Poe, though diverging sharply from that early romanticism in important respects. This was followed in the nineties by the Realistic revolt under Howells, in some of its aspects a return to the Eighteenth Century and the moralism of the Boston fathers, though some of its later and logical developments—the work of Dreiser for example—would have sent those fathers into convulsions. Finally, about 1915, we have the loudest and most startling of these revolutions, which is still too close to us to be labelled and ticketed with any certainty. Perhaps Radical Anarchism will do for a temporary name. We are still living in the smoke and thunder of this last revolution.

Running through all these changes, we find certain vitally important questions, which every critic has been forced to answer in some sense. These questions, as Professor Foerster has pointed out, are three in number:

1. What is the relation of literature to morality?
2. What is the relation of literature to reality?
3. What is the relation of American literature to the national spirit? [1]

To take only the last of these questions, we have seen that the attitude of the early North American school of critics was one of prophetic expectancy. There was as yet no American literature, but there

[1] Quoted from the introduction to *American Criticism,* by Norman Foerster (1928).

would be one. A country with such high mountains, such broad prairies, such deep rivers, could not fail to produce a great literature. The ridicule of Lowell sent this attitude into hiding for half a century. Lowell's own answer was that American literature, while possessing by his day a great deal of excellence, could not for a moment bear comparison with the great literatures of the past, not even with the contemporary literature of England; and as he grew older he came to esteem it less and less. Emerson, with sharper mind and sharper expression, declared roundly that American literature was secondary, derivative, wholly unrepresentative of the genuine American spirit. From Poe we have no such general pronouncement, though he clearly recognized and reproved the common American vice of overpraising the worthless. Stedman, though he had, I am convinced, a pretty clear notion of the comparative value of American writers, never spoke out. With him begins the era of complacency, of reverence for the great New England tradition. And in spite of Howells's unsparing condemnation of all writers who failed to conform to the infallible principles of realism, we find in him that same complacency repeated. The silence of Huneker is significant, but it was not until the work of John

Macy that we find the Emersonian dictum, that American literature is a feeble copy of English literature, once more plainly stated, but with this difference: by Macy's time certain American writers had appeared—Twain, Thoreau, Whitman—whom he recognized as genuinely American in spirit and in utterance. And there is this further difference to be observed; while the depreciations of Emerson and Lowell had no effect on general opinion, Macy's repetition of those depreciations has passed, for the time being at least, into current literary thought.

And now, in conclusion, may I be permitted to say a word by way of a plea of confession and avoidance. It was in 1922, in the course of a study of Lowell as a critic, that I first became aware of the lack, strange indeed in these days of theses without number, of any connected study of the course of literary criticism in America. No one seemed to know that there was an American literary criticism, or to have the faintest idea that any critic of importance, save Lowell, had ever written in America. With something of the zest of the explorer, therefore, I began to read in this field. Gradually, as I read, the pattern began to appear, and certain figures stood out from the pattern. That pattern, and those figures, is what I have here tried to present to the reader.

EPILOGUE

This book is just what its title signifies—a preliminary survey. It is therefore necessarily incomplete; it does not pretend to completeness. No one knows better than myself how much has been left out. I have conscientiously omitted Paul Elmer More because I wished to deal with no critic still living. I have left out John Burroughs, fine critic though he is, because he seems to me not quite of the first rank, and because he represents no general tendency. I have passed by, with a sigh of regret, Harry Thurston Peck and the *Bookman* of the nineties. I have, with a struggle, denied myself the pleasure of writing a chapter on Richard Grant White, greatest of American Shakespeare critics, and one of the greatest Shakespearian critics of all time. In all this my attempt has been to present, with unblurred outlines, a picture of the main course of literary criticism in America.

General Bibliography

A representative list of works by critics not treated at length in this study.

Babbitt, Irving	*Rousseau and Romanticism*	1919
Brownell, William C.	*American Prose Masters*	1909
Brooks, Van Wyck	*The Ordeal of Mark Twain*	1920
Burroughs, John	*Indoor Studies*	1889
	Whitman, a Study	1893
Cabell, James Branch	*Beyond Life*	1919
Crawford, F. Marion	*The Novel; What It Is*	1893
Hearn, Lafcadio	*Exotics and Retrospectives*	1899
Higginson, T. W.	*Margaret Fuller* (AML)	1844
Hudson, Henry Norman	*Shakespeare, His Life, Art, and Character*	1875
Lanier, Sidney	*The Science of English Verse*	1880
Longfellow, Henry Wadsworth	*Prose works,* 3 Vols.	1866
Mabie, Hamilton Wright	*Essays in Literary Interpretation*	1892
Macy, John	*The Spirit of American Literature*	1913
Matthews, Brander	*A Study of the Drama*	1910
	French Dramatists of the Nineteenth Century	1881
Mencken, Henry L.	*Prejudices,* Six series	1919–27
	A Book of Prefaces	1917
More, Paul Elmer	*Shelburne Essays,* 11 Vols.	1904
Perry, Bliss	*A Study of Poetry*	1920
Pattee, Fred L.	*American Literature Since 1870*	1915

Prescott, William Hickling	*Biographical and Critical Miscellanies*	1845
Repplier, Agnes	*Books and Men*	1888
Simms, William Gilmore	*Views and Reviews in American Literature*	1845
Spingarn, Joel Elias	*Creative Criticism*	1911
White, Richard Grant	*Studies in Shakespeare*	1886
	Memoirs of the Life of Shakespeare	1865
Whitman, Walt	*Democratic Vistas*	1875
	Preface to *Leaves of Grass*	1885
Woodberry, George E.	*Great Writers*	1912

INDEX

Ade, George, 194
Ainsworth, William Harrison, 99
Alciphron, 95
Aldrich, Thomas Bailey, 137
American Flag, The, 99
American Notes, 37
American Poetry, Criticism of, 26, 40, 126, 145-9
American Scholar, The, 122
Americans, 254-9
Among My Books, 56
Anastasius, 22
Anderson, Sherwood, 188, 272
Anna Karenina, 170
Anthology Club, 18
Arnold, Matthew, 77, 138, 141, 143, 159, 249, 251, 252, 253, 258
Arrowsmith, 268
Art of Fiction, The, 174
Atlantic Monthly, 57, 134, 183
Austen, Jane, 187, 190

Babbitt, Irving, 82, 226, 241, 247, 254
Balzac, Honoré de, 37, 130, 160, 168, 169
Baudelaire, Charles, 160, 162, 227
Beaumont and Fletcher, 78, 125
Becque, Henri, 240
Bedouins, 229
Beerbohm, Max, 93
Bennett, Arnold, 253
Books, 269
Boston, 17, 133, 203
Bourne, Randolph, 246
Bowen, Francis, 35-7
Boyd, Ernest, 242
Brooks, VanWyck, 128, 246
Brown, Charles Brockden, 17, 133
Brownell, William C., 226, 241, 247, 254
Browning, Elizabeth Barrett, 145
Browning, Robert, 55
Bryant, William Cullen, 26, 56, 91, 126, 145, 146
Bulwer, Edward, 55, 95
Burke, Edmund, 64
Burroughs, John, 128, 148, 281
Byron, Lord, 22, 23, 41, 42, 57, 130
Bysshe, Edward, 23

Cabell, James Branch, 190
Calverton, V. F., 128
Cambridge History of American Literature, 248
Campbell, Thomas, 22
Captain of the Gray Horse Troop, The, 202
Carlyle, Thomas, 33, 64, 125
Carter, Robert, 49
Century Magazine, 134
Channing, E. T., 21, 31
Channing, Walter, 18
Channing, William Ellery, 36
Character and Characteristic Men, 48
Chateaubriand, François René de, 64
Chaucer, Geoffrey, 24, 52, 72-3, 74, 82
Classicism, 65-9, 120, 222
Coleridge, Samuel Taylor, 22, 28, 32, 43, 121
Conrad, Joseph, 234
Conversations on Some of the Old Poets, 48, 52, 106
Conway, Moncure D., 148
Cooper, James Fenimore, 17, 27, 36, 98, 130, 201
Crabbe, George, 33
Crane, Stephen, 194, 197
Critical Woodcuts, 270-4
Criticism, Theories of, 52, 53, 58, 98, 102, 103, 123-4, 225-7, 270
Crumbling Idols, 202-4
Curtis, George William, 198

Dana, Richard Henry, 18, 21, 28-9, 31, 32, 40, 52, 277
d'Annunzio, Gabriel, 240
Dante, 72, 74, 82
Defence of Poesie, 33
Demetrius, 22
Democracy and Other Addresses, 258

INDEX

Dickens, Charles, 37, 64, 96, 125, 186
D'Israeli, Benjamin, 55, 266
Doyle, Arthur Conan, 202
Drake, Joseph Rodman, 89, 99
Drama, Criticism of the, 105-7, 236
Dreiser, Theodore, 188, 250
Dryden, John, 66
Dumas, Alexandre, 37, 160

Edgeworth, Maria, 22
Edinburg Review, 18, 19, 25
Egoists, 229
Eighteenth Century, 23, 32, 53, 76, 89, 277
Eliot, George, 170
Ellis, Havelock, 236
Emerson, Ralph Waldo, 32, 33, 36, 56, 118-28, 130, 131, 235, 241, 246, 257, 279
Eureka, 258
Evangeline, 140
Everett, A. H., 18, 21, 22, 25, 31, 33
Everett, Edward, 21

Fable for Critics, A, 55
Faerie Queene, The, 69
Fall of the House of Usher, The, 54, 93
Fashion, 108
Felton, C. C., 33, 36
Fielding, Henry, 61
Flaubert, Gustave, 160, 229
Foerster, Norman, 69, 70, 278
France, Anatole, 229, 233
Franklin, Benjamin, 257
French Literature, 25, 34, 212, 236
French Poets and Novelists, 159
Fuller, Margaret, 56, 128-31

Gammer Gurton's Needle, 62
Gardiner, John Sylvester, 27
Garland, Hamlin, 201-4
Gautier, Theophile, 160, 169-70
Genius and Other Essays, 135
Genius of America, The, 258-62
Georgia Scenes, 96
Goethe, Johann Wolfgang von, 119, 125
Gorky, Maxim, 234, 236, 240
Graham's Magazine, 44, 53, 86
Gray, Thomas, 76
Greene, Robert, 78
Greenwood, F. W. P., 29-30
Griswold, Rufus, 40
Guy Fawkes, 99

Hadad, 30
Harper's Magazine, 183, 190
Harvard College, 18, 19, 56, 248
Hauptmann, Gerhard, 236, 240
Hawthorne, Nathaniel, 32, 126, 131, 160, 170, 257
Hawthorne (Life by James), 159
Hazlitt, William, 28
Higginson, T. W., 129
Hillhouse, James, 30
Holmes, Oliver Wendell, 32
Homeward Bound, 36
Hope Leslie, 31
Horseshoe Robinson, 91
Howells, William Dean, 134, 173, 178, 180, 182-98, 229, 246, 277, 279
Hugo, Victor, 78, 160
Humanism, 82, 241, 247
Huneker, James G., 159, 206-44, 275, 279
Huntly, Lydia, 19
Hyperion, 99

Ibsen, Henrik, 223-4, 240
Iconoclasts, 229, 236, 239
In Memoriam, 125
Irving, Washington, 17, 29, 56, 126
Italian Literature, 34

James, G. P. R., 99
James, Henry, 87, 134, 158-81, 182, 184, 187, 195, 227, 230, 235, 241, 252
Joyce, James, 236

Kavanaugh, 55
Keats, John, 22, 43, 52, 56, 57
Kipling, Rudyard, 170
Kittredge, George Lyman, 82

Lamartine, Alphonse de, 64
Landor, Walter Savage, 143
Latest Literary Essays and Addresses, 58, 75
Lawrence, D. H., 188, 272
Lectures on the Age of Elizabeth, 47
Les Miserables, 233
Lewis, Sinclair, 247, 266-8

INDEX

Library of Old Authors, 71
Linwoods, The, 31
Literary Friends and Acquaintance, 188
Literary History of America, 245
Literature and Life, 48
Longfellow, Henry Wadsworth, 32, 33-5, 40, 55, 90, 99, 126, 130, 139, 246, 277
Longstreet, George, 96
Lowell, James Russell, 32, 36, 38, 49-85, 86-8, 93, 113, 118, 126, 127, 131, 134, 137, 159, 183, 246, 258, 277, 279

Mabie, Hamilton Wright, 81
Macaulay, Thomas B., 39, 96, 125
Macy, John, 128, 185, 246, 280
Mademoiselle de Maupin, 162
Maeterlinck, Maurice, 218, 240
Maggie, 197
Main Travelled Roads, 197
Marlowe, Christopher, 78
Marryat, Frederick, 98
Massinger, Philip, 79
Masters, Edgar Lee, 247
Matthew Arnold: How to Know Him, 248
Matthews, Brander, 114
Maupassant, Guy de, 160, 162, 165-6
Mencken, H. L., 80, 114, 242, 246, 247, 248, 256-7, 273-4
Mezzotints in Modern Music, 218
Middleton, Thomas, 50
Milton, John, 120
Montaigne, Michel de, 125
Moore, George, 236, 250
Moore, Thomas, 22, 95, 130
Moral Pieces in Prose and Verse, 19
Morality and Literature, 24, 30, 34, 38, 68, 129-30, 136-7, 151, 162, 165-7, 183-5, 208-11, 226-7, 253
More, Paul Elmer, 247, 281
Motley, John Lothrop, 37-8
Mowatt, Cora, 108
Musset, Alfred de, 160
My Dear Cornelia, 268-9
My Literary Passions, 187
My Study Windows, 58

Nathan, George Jean, 246
Naturalism, 249
Nature and Elements of Poetry, The, 135, 150
Newman, John Henry, 229
New York, 131, 133, 204
New York Mirror, 44
Nietzsche, Friedrich, 236
Norris, Frank, 194, 198-202
Norris, Kathleen, 195
North American Review, 17-47, 49, 53, 71, 95, 127, 136
Norton, Andrews, 30
Norton, Charles E., 82
Notes on Novelists, 159
Novel, Criticism of the, 27, 37, 160, 168-77, 183-7, 198-202

Octopus, The, 197
Ode to a Nightingale, The, 52
Old English Dramatists, The, 48, 75, 77-80
On Contemporary Literature, 249
Opinions of a Literary Radical, The, 256
Ordeal of Mark Twain, The, 256
Ordeal of Richard Feverel, The, 170

Palfrey, John Gorham, 18, 21
Partial Portraits, 159, 178
Pater, Walter, 229
Peabody, Oliver W. B., 30, 32, 33
Peabody, William B. O., 30, 32
Peck, Harry Thurston, 281
Peele, George, 78
Percival, James Gates, 70
Petrarch, Francis, 64
Phillips, Willard, 18, 26, 31
Philosophy of Composition, The, 87, 110
Pinkney, Edward C., 30, 40
Pioneer, The, 49-51
Poe, Edgar Allan, 36, 53, 56, 86-117, 118, 126, 127, 131, 152, 163-4, 173, 179, 230, 235, 246, 258, 277, 279
Poetic Principle, The, 87, 110
Poets and Poetry of America, The, 40
Poets of America, 135, 145
Points of View, 263-7
Poole, Ernest, 194
Pope, Alexander, 23, 52, 62
Powhatan, 98
Prejudices, 115
Prescott, William Hickling, 25, 33
Psalm of Life, The, 40

Rationale of Verse, The, 87, 112
Realism, 61, 121-2, 172-7, 185-7, 191-3, 196, 198-202, 241, 277
Reilly, J. J., 80
Responsibilities of the Novelist, The, 198
Ripley, George, 131
Romanticism in America, 28, 44, 51, 57, 60, 89, 121, 191-3, 220, 277
Rousseau, Jean J., 64
Rousseau and Romanticism, 82
Ruskin, John, 64

Sainte-Beuve, Charles Auguste, 159, 228
Saintsbury, George, 40, 88
Saltus, Edgar, 235
Sand, George, 162, 170
Scott, Walter, 20, 21, 22, 23
Scribe, Eugene, 239
Sedgwick, Catherine, 31
Shakespeare, William, 24, 27, 78, 125
Shaw, George Bernard, 229, 230, 238, 240
Shelley, Percy Bysshe, 22, 41, 130, 251
Sherman, Stuart P., 177, 245-76
Shorey, Paul, 254
Sidney, Philip, 33
Smith, Seba, 98
Smith, Sydney, 41
Southern Literary Messenger, The, 43
Southey, Robert, 95
Spanish Student, The, 40, 90
Sparks, Jared, 21, 31
Spenser, Edmund, 24, 43
Spirit of American Literature, The, 246
Spoon River Anthology, The, 247
Spy, The, 27
Standards, 256
Stedman, Edmund Clarence, 114, 133-57, 179, 180, 184, 230, 277, 279
Steeplejack, 224, 231
Stendhal, Henri Beyle, 230
Stevenson, Robert Louis, 170
Strindberg, August, 240
Sudermann, Hermann, 240
Sue, Eugene, 130, 160
Swinburne, Algernon Charles, 143
Synge, John Millington, 251

Taine, Hippolyte Adolphe, 42
Talfourd, Thomas, 39
Tarkington, Booth, 194
Taylor, Bayard, 137, 145
Tennyson, Alfred, 95, 125, 143
Thackeray, William Makepeace, 186
Thanatopsis, 26
Theocritus, 143
Thoreau, Henry David, 67, 127, 235, 246
Ticknor, George, 81
Tolstoy, Leo, 160, 190, 202, 239
Tower of London, The, 99
Trilby, 198
Trollope, Anthony, 169, 170, 190
Tudor, William, 18-21, 23, 49
Turgeniev, Ivan, 160, 170
Twain, Mark, 246, 251
Twice-Told Tales, 32, 33

Unicorns, 229

Van Doren, Carl, 128, 246
Van Vechten, Carl, 235
Veritism, 203
Victorian Poets, 135, 142
Vision of Rubeta, The, 99
Voltaire, François Marie Arouet de, 23

Warner, Charles Dudley, 198
Waterston, R. C., 33
Webster, John, 78
Wedekind, Frank, 234
Wells, Herbert George, 250, 252, 272
Wendell, Barrett, 245
Wharton, Edith, 194, 229
Whipple, Edwin Percy, 38-43, 47-8
White, Richard Grant, 133, 281
Whitlock, Brand, 195
Whitman, Walt, 123, 128, 147-8, 229, 235, 246, 257
Whittier, John Greenleaf, 32, 41, 56, 140, 246
Wilde, Oscar, 272
Willis, Nathaniel P., 131, 133
Woodberry, George E., 81, 152
Wordsworth, William, 22, 28, 29, 41, 57, 63, 73, 121
Wyatt, Edith, 195

Yamoyden, a Tale, 22

Zola, Emile, 61, 160, 170, 229, 234

THE LAMP AND THE LUTE

This edition published by
Frank Cass and Co Ltd
10 Woburn Walk London WC1
by arrangement with Oxford University Press

First published 1929
Second edition 1964

Printed by Thomas Nelson (Printers) Ltd
London ann Edinburgh